Malcolm Quantrill

Ritual and Response in Architecture

Lund Humphries   London

In memory of my teacher and friend, Ernst Wiesner, born Brno 1890, died Liverpool 1971.

'Man is indeed the only animal to leave records behind him, for he is the only animal whose products "recall to mind" an idea distinct from their material existence. Other animals use signs and contrive structures, but they use signs without "perceiving the relation of signification", and they contrive structures without perceiving the relation of construction.

'To perceive the relation of signification is to separate the idea of the concept to be expressed from the means of expression. And to perceive the relation of construction is to separate the idea of the function to be fulfilled from the means of fulfilling it.

'Man's signs and structures are records because, or rather in so far as, they express ideas separated from, yet realized by, the process of signalling and building.'

Erwin Panofsky
Meaning in the Visual Arts

Photographic Acknowledgements

The illustrations on pages 127 to 142 are taken from photographs by the author, with the exception of the following:

Figures 1 and 4: *The New Churches of Europe* by G. E. Kidder Smith.
Figure 2: Ahrends Burton and Koralek, London (photograph by Walter Rawlings).
Figure 6: Bibliothèque nationale, Paris.
Figure 9: Picturepoint Ltd, London.
Figure 10: Prestel Verlag, Munich.
Figure 14: Greater London Council.
Figure 16: *From Schinkel to the Bauhaus* by Julius Posener.
Figure 18: Rijksmuseum voor Volkenkunde, Leiden, Holland.
Figure 19: A. F. Kersting, London.
Figures 21 and 22: *Monde grec* (*Architecture universelle*) by Roland Martin, Office du Livre, Fribourg (photograph by Henri Stierlin).
Figure 23: London Midland Region, British Rail.
Figure 24: London Transport Executive.

Contents

Foreword

These essays began to take shape when Professor Robert Gardner-Medwin asked me to give a series of lectures in the second year theory course at the Liverpool School of Architecture. The intention was to replace a conventional survey of the literature of architectural theory by a broader framework of reference against which the student might measure the doubts and anxieties that currently surround architectural education and practice.

During my stay in America my thoughts were particularly stimulated by Dean G. Holmes Perkins of the University of Pennsylvania, Professor Rudolph Heberle of Louisiana State University, and Louis Kahn. Since that time I have been further prompted by Dean Bertram Berenson, Professor Henry-Russell Hitchcock, Ken Garland and Reima Pietila, and the late John Bailey and Anton Ehrenzweig. The idea of collecting the essays was touched off by an invitation to give two public lectures sponsored by the St Albans School of Art, resulting in the original versions of 'Architect – man and myth: aspects of a dilemma' and 'When the elephants were white!', and a request from Anthony Davis, editor of *Building*, that he might publish my notes in article form.

Those original notes must have been a curious experience for my students, many of whom seemed to have imagined that I was giving a remedial course in aesthetics. I have therefore welcomed the opportunity for revision.

These essays, now substantially different from the original articles, remain, however, based on my lectures. Whatever the disadvantages of the architectural lecture in conveying the imagination and power of actual buildings the visual footnote of the slide is an invaluable aid. It is difficult to reproduce that immediacy in a book of limited dimensions but my publishers have been most constructive in aiding my efforts to surmount this difficulty.

My thanks are due to Ljiljana Momcilovic who provided the original drawings for the articles, some of which are included again here. Also, I must record my debt to the library of the Architectural Association, and particularly the AA's librarian, Elizabeth Dixon. Dr Melvin Dalgarno, of Aberdeen University, also read the text in draft and made many helpful suggestions for its improvement for which I am particularly grateful. My warmest thanks are also due to my wife who assisted me in the project in every possible way.

Finally, although points made in some essays are counterpointed in others it has not been my method or intention, in arranging the essays in their present form, to produce a single progression of argument from one topic to another. I have rather attempted to maintain a peripheral attack on the architecture (the symbolic environment) as a whole than try to arrive at conclusions or solutions. Some of the material was originally prepared for students of architecture and some for a wider audience. It is my hope that the present text will find readers among all those interested in the cause and effect of the environmental image.

Malcolm Quantrill

Preface

As a teacher of architectural history, I find it embarrassing that lectures on the evolution of architectural styles remain a central part of architectural education today. Of course history in this form is a truly academic subject and has real value as such; also it serves as a reminder of the qualities of previous societies and civilizations, qualities which produced varied and ingenious solutions to the formal problems of building in particular periods. But history lectures which catalogue in two or three years the fashions and styles of architecture from Tutankhamun to Trotsky cannot provide the anatomy and physiology of building art and science, yet they often constitute the only comprehensive and cohesive menu in a course that is mostly made up of technical side-dishes.

What is then the objective of the historical exercise? Is it still presumed that no good architect will emerge other than from the architectural tradition, in the same way that all good writers are presumed to emerge from the literary tradition? If so, just what is this tradition: is it national, regional, or cultural? Nobody seems quite sure, and in the supposedly healthy atmosphere of universal doubt the methodical historian continues for the most part to practise the funereal art of embalming dead forms, which are then displayed in endless lines on the great cultural lantern show. We may have shed some vestiges of the École des Beaux-Arts but this aspect of the 'sentimental journey' still remains in architectural education.

I am not suggesting for a moment that mystery is not an essential component in the design of the built environment. Rationalism may be part of the puzzle, but it is only a part, and if I have to take sides I must declare myself a mystic rather than a rationalist in these matters.

The mystery of architecture is to be found in one's own relationship with it, whether as architect or layman. My fear concerning the traditional teaching of architectural history is that it often conspires to remove this sense of mystery. The great lantern show of the architectural history lecture, whatever the intention, emerges as a nostalgic search for *les temps perdus*. When I began my studies as an articled pupil the Second World War had not long been over and the number of books on architectural history was limited. By 1960, however, this shortage no longer obtained and today the student can pursue private study by reading from a wide range of texts and commentaries and the formal lecture has, as a consequence, outlived its value. What is needed instead is a programme of contexts within which form and style can be assessed in relation to cultural contents.

Recently Golo Mann wrote: 'I always regarded history lectures at university as nonsensical and as a student I never listened to one; as a Professor in German universities I came to grief on the futility of this method of teaching. It was valid before Johannes Gutenberg, but not for the last five hundred years. The students ought to read at home. The two hours of class (or however many it is) must be used for the discussion of the reading matter.'[1]

It is my intention in this collection of essays to introduce contexts and explore relationships, ranging widely over the architect's source material and the influences that are brought to bear upon him. In this task I have given myself considerable freedom to manoeuvre within the framework of ritual, myth, form, and style.

Today there is hardly an institution or custom that is not being continually investigated to determine its validity in the past, the present, and the future. Do we any longer need literature or the theatre? And what about professors, parliaments, churches, schools, lessons, grammar, and so on? It is therefore only natural that architects and architecture too have come under scrutiny. What does a profession so obviously rooted in history and the history of its own exclusiveness have to offer the societies of today and the future? I have tried to come at these questions from different points of view, with the aim of stimulating further discussion and enquiry. The very complexity of architecture forbids any simple formulae or solutions.

Peter Cook in his book *Architecture: action and plan* states: 'As architecture is a social art the value of a building must lie chiefly in its ability to create environment out of human situations'. Later he warns us that 'The process of forming the building comes from the abstractness of a series of ideas at one end, a series of constraints at the other, and any number of variable (and often incoherently devised) briefing points between'. He continues by explaining that 'The architect is in the ambiguous position of looking after his clients' interests – and yet retaining the creative and professional isolation which can produce the best building possible. But we are culturally and technologically in a state of transition, and his role is becoming more and more ambiguous as the number of variables of control, technique, and involvement of other specialists increases. The "architect-cum-master-craftsman" could control the whole process, and therefore the quality of the building was entirely up to him. Now he must be much more of a synthesiser, an interpreter. This might not ultimately negate his role – it just gives architects certain uncomfortable growing pains at the present.'

It is easy enough to quarrel with some of Cook's speculations, but I am grateful to him for expressing the situation so lucidly and unemotionally. It might be useful at the same time to link his observations with some made recently at the Liverpool School by Christopher Jones. Speaking to the topic 'Does architecture have a future?' Jones said: 'In answering the question "Will the architect survive?" we could say that any specialisation, and consequently any specialist, is always in danger of becoming outmoded. But it seems to me that architecture is so vague an activity that it cannot be defined and that which cannot be isolated cannot be eliminated.' Later he added: 'Architects know how to live: they have a highly developed sense of life-style. They know where to eat and what to drink. This life-style permeates their homes, which are more often than not Georgian or skilfully converted Victorian houses rather than new buildings. But they are not particularly successful at passing on this life-style to the rest of society, at educating others in their way of life. To a certain extent this educational role is being fulfilled by the women's magazines.'

I believe that these statements of Jones, in their deceptively loose way, provide a means of examining where architecture in our society seems to fail. Firstly, Jones suggests that it is non-specific. My own view is that this is because as an activity it has no ritual attachment to our society. In other words the profession becomes confused about its role when architects fail to identify the main ritual patterns of our society and, as a consequence, fail to respond to these in formal terms.

The second inference in Jones's remarks is that architects have benefited from their education because it allows them to amalgamate selected elements from the societies of previous periods into their own idiosyncratic life-style. There is a further implication that this life-style is compounded of the gourmet on the one hand and a certain over-indulgent skill at interior decoration on the other.

It is, of course, common in history to find one society borrowing the styles and manners of another, but examples are usually exclusive to one source in any one period. The Romans borrowed from the Greeks, the Elizabethans emulated Italian dress and the French masons of Francis I effected the Italian style in their decorative treatments. Since the end of the eighteenth century, however, when first the Neoclassical and then the Romantic movements paralleled the Industrial Revolution, architects have been inclined to draw upon a number and variety of sources at any one time. For example, Le Corbusier's Ronchamp chapel is a blend of ship's cowls and Paul Klee faces, the New Library at Trinity College, Dublin, is credible only as a disinterred bunker with Gothic hood moulds, while the Household Cavalry's new headquarters is a loose-knit Sanmichele sandwich with extra frills by courtesy of an untamed resident (Figs.1, 2, 3).

Le Corbusier was himself severely critical of fashion in design, although he referred to it as stylism. 'You don't know anything about the "Orders" nor the "1925 style"; and if I catch you designing in the 1925 style, I'll box your ears. You must not be a stylist. You articulate, you plan, nothing more.' And again: 'Architecture is organisation. YOU ARE AN ORGANISER, NOT A DRAWING BOARD STYLIST.'[2] The main ingredient missing from his Marseilles Unité (Fig.4) was an understanding of the ritual that generates an urban life-style. For this reason the Unité did not catch on with French people: its apartments rented slowly and this pace was not improved by the reluctance of the French shopkeepers to take over shopping units so remote from the traditional street level, i.e., the *rez-de-chaussée*. It might be argued by some that the Unité was, in this respect, ahead of its time, but it was Le Corbusier's specific brief to help solve the housing shortage not to provide a Mecca for the eccentric intellectuals who eventually occupied most of the apartments, assembling a kind of Human Zoo where we could observe ourselves in all our Ionescoesque absurdity.

Le Corbusier should have realized that a Versailles tipped up on end, with its garden on the roof, threw away the advantages of corridor and gallery, those vital lanes of human communication which were the living heart of Louis XIV's palace. Thus the Unité became an example of architectural fashion, i.e., style not supported by a relevant ritual, and this fashion was readily imported into Britain in the form of tower-block housing. It is easy to see how a fashion, which, with its roof-garden, was barely supportable as a concept in the coastal Mediterranean climate, became a ridiculous affectation when subject to the heavy rainful and industrial pollution of English urban sites.

If architecture is then an organizational, problem-solving activity it is clear that, in spite of Cook's scepticism about the 'variable' and 'incoherently devised briefing points', we should aim at getting the problem clearly stated before we attempt to solve it and not the other way about. One obvious obstacle to this sort of clarity is the way in which rituals have proliferated in our society. This profusion and resulting confusion has been used in some quarters as an argument to justify the proliferation of architectural fashions in twentieth-century work.[3] Perhaps twentieth-century architecture has been rather more a matter of fashion imposing ritualistic patterns on building users instead of the more logical evolution of form from ritual: for example a Hall of Residence for a red-brick university conceived on a collegiate pattern when no such pattern exists in the real life of the Hall (Fig.5).

Christopher Alexander's Centre for Urban Structures seems to be concerned with just such an evolutionary approach to planning problems, accepting that ritual is the generator of plans which in turn generate architectural form, the plan being 'the footprint of the building' as Louis Kahn has reminded us. The Centre for Urban Structures made proposals in the Projecto Experimental Competition for housing to be built at Lima in Peru, and these proposals embodied a useful example of their working methods. As they were designing for low-income families Alexander and his colleagues each lived with a Peruvian family in that social strata. Then,

using the classical field-work techniques of the social anthropologist, they plotted the behavioural patterns (rituals) of these families. This allowed them to establish the car–pedestrian symbiosis, an intimacy gradient within the dwellings (from the 'public' formal area closest to the entrance through to the more intimate and private informal areas at the rear) and a pattern for bed-clusters based on the segregation of boys from girls with the parents' bedroom placed between the children's areas.

This systematic approach by the c u s produced an analysis of ritual that allowed a solution relating each individual bedspace to the neighbourhood pattern as a whole. The studies undertaken by the c u s give room for some optimism about the future of design strategy, and they demonstrate quite clearly the difference between Le Corbusier's superimposed forms and Alexander's concern with anthropological factors. If such studies were always undertaken we might avoid the consequences of uprooting central urban populations and decanting them to remote suburban sites where they have none of the facilities or environmental associations of their previous way of life. But such an approach has its prerequisite, an understanding that people's bedrooms, living rooms, and back-gardens have at least an equal value in the decision-making process with the motorway and the airport, with pre-emptive rights and privileges *hors de concours*; in other words the acceptance of the political motive in the design process. Although Peter Land persuaded the Peruvian Government and the u n to promote a competition which provided an opportunity for a more detailed look at low-cost housing than governments normally allow, we have yet to receive evidence that this competition will benefit low-cost housing in Peru in general or Latin America as a whole.

If we can still accept 'commodity, firmness and delight' as the three essential criteria of architecture (Cook prefers 'performance, identity and economy of means') our present-day achievements leave quite a lot to be desired. We have a multiplicity of 'systems' but no longer is there an overall discipline to develop our sense of space, structural integrity and spirit of joy. Classical, Byzantine and Gothic architecture had such disciplines. Today there is no simple solution, but our failures to integrate commodity, firmness and delight are a fact, and the multiplicity of variables is not an excuse. Our dilemma, I suggest, is based on the lack of correlation between ritual and building form, as a consequence of which form in architecture has come to have only a limited significance; it too often depends only upon the arbitrariness of fashion, and it is part of my aim to discuss this arbitrariness in relation to the ritual and style of contrasting societies and periods.

Architect – man and myth: aspects of a dilemma

It has often been the role of academies to perpetuate outmoded stylistic expression, the maintenance of so-called traditional forms and details, long after the traditions from which they sprang have ceased to be a valid component of a culture. For the purposes of my present argument I should like to consider the support we give through the various institutions of society for these 'traditions' as a malfunction of myth. For various reasons we have made a habit of taking a legend together with its framework of formal language, reinterpreting it and transplanting it to another place and another time. Steiner speaks of the coherence of a thing being harmonic with time. T. S. Eliot commented on this 'coherence' in his poem *Ash Wednesday*:

Because I know that time is always time
And place is always and only place
And what is actual is actual only for one time
And only for one place.[1]

It is perhaps significant that the Beatles, much photographed with the ascetic and hopefully venerable Maharishi, ultimately chose as the trade mark for their own commercial company an apple, that seductive symbol which is synonomous with sin and transgression in the Western world, thus deliberately setting themselves against the whole Judaic-Christian world. Of course, it could be argued that it was about time that the concept of 'sin' was depersonalized in our society, but the central problem of responsibility remains and must remain one for the individual. I believe that basically the younger generation wants love and security, whilst inevitably sampling Browning's 'dangerous edge of things', and seeks the orgy, the pleasures of *plage*, with the same desperation and boredom that characterized the 1930s. Lonely, without a sense of community or 'divine purpose', they seek dark places in which to hide and commune with ancient gods: theirs is a romantic gesture in the extreme, since they yearn not merely for the immediate past but for the ultimate past.

Carson Pirie Scott store, Chicago (1899–1906) by Louis Sullivan, D. H. Burnham and Company.

G. S. Kirk asserts that 'There is no one definition of myth, no Platonic form of a myth against which all actual instances can be measured'.[2] He maintains that myths differ enormously in their morphology and social function. I wish to consider myth from the point of view of abstracting values, symbols and even rituals from previous societies. Kirk attacks the idea that all myths are associated with rituals, and the even narrower view that they all originated from rituals 'for which they offer a motive or cause', saying: 'This theory had an astonishing vogue from the time when it was first acquired (from Robertson Smith and Frazer for the most part) by Biblical scholars, who saw that it had a certain attraction in relation to the myths of the Near East, and in particular could make theologically acceptable sense of some of the Hebrew material.' It is undoubtedly the case that many myths, perhaps especially in the Near East, were associated with rituals, and that some of them may have been created to account for actions whose purpose was no longer apparent. Yet it is often difficult to tell, from the form of the myth and the ritual alone, which came first, and caution is necessary . . . The words of a careful critic, R. de Langhe, are salutary: 'while the study of the myths and ritual practices of so-called primitive peoples has in some cases revealed a close relationship between myths and rituals, it is equally true that it has also shown the existence of myths which are unaccompanied by any ritual performance. Between these two extremes many intermediate types can be attested.'

My principal concern in these reflections is, however, to show the relationship of ritual to the form or style of buildings and groups of buildings. For this reason I shall be returning to the consideration of myth and ritual as causal concept (see p.63). Certainly the academies, growing out of French Neoclassicism, may be blamed for the persistent imposition of outmoded fashions in architectural expression: this imposition of mostly irrelevant forms and details on modern buildings has continued by way of academic architectural education. It was against just such irrelevant formalism that Louis Sullivan argued and wrote, for example in *Autobiography of an Idea*.

Sullivan in fact only succeeded in advancing one decorative system as a replacement for another but we cannot blame him for that: his reaction was limited by the limitations of his education and environmental experience and the problems of resolving technological dualities (the steel-framed building clad in masonry and other traditional material) into a new formalism. But his intention, at least, was anti-academic. Ledoux's intention was, I suggest, similarly anti-academic: his use of the classical vocabulary and the Palladian elements went beyond the 'comic' or 'absurd' effects of the Mannerists (Fig.6). One is not so much disturbed by Ledoux's proposals as excited by them. They must be seen more as projections of a future rather than as mere echoes of a past. Yet his forms were traditional ones, even classical ones, so that at best his intentions were, in the face of the advances in technology that paralleled their inception, rather romantic. Perhaps the difference may best be expressed by saying that while the ideal of Classicism is presented as a possible goal and one according to which man and society can be improved in a series of orderly stages, the Romantic artist pits himself against a basically hostile set of values and envisages the unattainable, an ideal beyond the possibilities of human adaptability.[3] The key ideas of the Romantic Movement are indicated by the words 'genius', 'creative imagination', 'originality', 'expression', 'communication', 'symbolism', 'emotion' and 'sentiment'. These concepts had been merely peripheral before the advent of the Romantic Movement, which gave them central importance as part of a totality, giving art in turn new functions and new standards of assessment. Furthermore, whereas Romantic Art is no longer in vogue and the more articulate ideas of the Romantic Movement are suspect, many of the assumptions to which the movement gave rise still survive in current art theory and continue to flourish in the language of criticism. In the Romantic Age the artist was no longer a man inspired by gods, but was himself elevated to the status of a hero or demi-god. The notion of genius as exceptional intellectual and spiritual endowment (not merely exceptional talent or skill in a particular direction), though not restricted to the arts, came to be associated more particularly with the concept of 'artist'. Genius from the time of the Romantic Movement has come to be connected especially with artistic activity; and although it may be achieved only by a few fortunate practitioners of the arts, it is still considered to be the natural condition to which all artists should aspire. Sometimes the artist-genius was thought of as having exceptional insight into ultimate reality or as himself being in some special sense an embodiment or manifestation of the absolute spirit revered by the German idealistic philosophers; even so the artist was thought to enjoy this special relation to reality by virtue of his own unique, natural endowments (see p.80). This surely describes our position in architectural education until quite recently if not actually at the present time.

In the late eighteenth and early nineteenth centuries the notion of genius was closely linked with that of originality. This Romantic theory of genius was concerned not with conforming to rules with more than average skill and efficiency but instead with the discovery of new rules and with effecting a breakthrough which would be accepted by subsequent generations of artists as the source of new avenues of exploration or modified rules. A genius must be essentially an original man. Kant argues that 'Fine art is only possible as a product of genius; originality must be its primary property'. The German philosopher felt that everyone was agreed 'on the point of the complete opposition between genius and the spirit of imitation'. Here we can identify the essential conflict between the Romantic spirit and the academic tradition in architecture. The academies were performing a purely reproductive function, teaching students to emulate this system or the other, to acquire an understanding of the rules necessary for the co-ordination of the established elements of architecture – whether they be the constituent parts of a classical Order or the modern

Carson Pirie Scott store, Chicago (1899–1906)
by Louis Sullivan, D. H. Burnham and Company.
Detail of front entrance.

definition of elements, i.e. floors, walls, roof, etc. – whereas those passing through this academic reproductive system have considered themselves (in error) to be privileged creators of original works, geniuses.

Thus our current dilemma arises from the conflict of academic intent (or limitation) with the Romantic Ideal. It has given rise to the myth of the architect as the oracle rather than the servant of the gods, or more importantly Man. Consequently the architect is now in the embarrassing position of a priest who is compelled to explain his god and his sacerdotal function to a rationalist. The problem is not one of determining whether it is the priest or the rationalist that is right, it is rather a question of persuading both that they have taken up false positions relative to the complex and varied needs of Man. Perhaps it was this that Frank Lloyd Wright had in mind when he quoted Lao Tse as saying: 'The reality of the building does not consist of walls and roof but in the space within that is to be lived in'. This is surely a very early example of existential thought as it relates to space. It is useful to examine Lao Tse's proposition because it defines architecture as the product of necessity, the formal response to the basic patterns of life: it describes a correspondence between living patterns and the expression of those patterns in a formal style. Also it describes the generation of form by the enclosure of space, rather than an inhibition of space by formal enclosure. In other words, architecture being the product of necessity grows from within: its impact on exterior space, the space between buildings, is a direct consequence of satisfying this interior need. The organization of exterior spaces will stem from the pattern of communication between individual units on the one hand and the organic growth of those units on the other. This is exactly what happens in the hill villages of the Greek Cycladic islands; there, the indigenous pattern formation is so strong that even classical elements ('moulding, by orderly stages towards an improved condition') such as churches which are superimposed on the indigenous structure are readily absorbed by the catalytic nature of the overall pattern (Fig.7). The classical grid-iron pattern is, of course, the very antithesis of the indigenous tradition in that its superstructure dictates the spatial relationships of the interstices rather than the other way about. Richelieu, that unique example of a classical town plan executed throughout in the same style, demonstrates this point well (Fig.8). Valletta, on the other hand, gains variety within the grid by virtue of its terrain (Figs.9, 10).

I believe it is significant that the rigid grid patterns on which 'primitive' modern prefabricated building component assemblies are based inhibit spatial organization by their very nature. I speak of component assemblies because it seems logical that a building 'system' should permit the spatial generation of form, rather than restrict the natural expression of space by the abstract formalization of elements. When I asked about his attitude to building systems and planning modules, Alvar Aalto said: 'The space is the system and the brick is the module'. Unfortunately, 'systems' as we mainly understand them tend to be a product of restrictive rules of design in the classical sense (see pp.49–51) rather than conceptualising frameworks.

Gjerløv-Knudsen[4] argues that science and technology have demonstrated a division between 'natural' and 'artificial' design: this is a parallel to the distinction between the indigenous and classical traditions in architecture. He proposes: 'It would be expedient in this connection to classify the various kinds of equipment used by plants, animals and man in their struggle for life against their surroundings. This equipment may be sub-divided into three categories: (1) Incorporated, (2) Accessory and (3) Liberated. As regards Incorporated equipment used by plants, we might mention their organs of respiration; as Accessory the tendrils; as Liberated equipment, the organs employed to expedite the spreading of their seed. As Incorporated equipment of animals, we might instance their prehensile organs; as Accessory, their horns and tusks; and as Liberated, their nests and dwellings. While in Man we might exemplify his sensory organs as Incorporated, his tools as Accessories, and his machines, vehicles, scientific and artistic production, as well as organising abilities, as Liberated.' He goes on to describe the 'Direct use of Form' in architecture, fine arts, crafts, industry, agriculture and the 'Indirect use of Form' in music, literature, the sciences and the humanities. Then he speaks of the 'Positional Relationship between Form-Function and Man' as either (1) objective, (2) objective-subjective, or (3) subjective. As objective he cites: automation, motive power, machines, vehicles, hidden services systems; as objective-subjective he cites: architecture, town planning, landscaping, furniture; as subjective he cites: crafts, sculptures, painting, music, poetry, science, modes of perception. There is, he argues, no sharp distinction between the objective-subjective and the purely subjective.

This in Gjerløv-Knudsen's terms would give us a formula for architecture as a liberated, objective-subjective, direct form system, and that would appear to have more connexion with the indigenous tradition than the classical tradition. It is ironical, therefore, that the grid-iron plan, the most adaptable in the long-term, is the most indeterminate, because of the flexibility of reorganization it permits. Vitruvius, at the very root of the classical academic tradition, already describes the divorce between ritual and form in Book 1:5: 'A wide knowledge of history is requisite because, among the ornamental part of an architect's design for a work, there are many the underlying idea of whose employment he should be able to explain to the enquirers. For instance, suppose him to set up the marble statues of women in long robes, called Caryatides, to take the place of columns, with the mutules and coronas placed directly above their heads, he will give the following explanation to his questioners. Caryae, a state in Peloponnesus, sided with the Persian enemies against Greece; later the Greeks, having gloriously won their freedom by victory in war . . . declared war against the people of Caryae. They took the town, killed the men . . . and carried off the women into slavery, without permitting them however to lay aside the long robes and other marks of their rank as married women, so that they might be obliged to appear forever after burdened with the weight of their shame.'[5] In other words it was already necessary in Vitruvius's day for an architect to acquire knowledge of so-called tradition, and exercise the malfunction of myth by translating the formal language of another society and another time to his own.

In the indigenous (or anonymous) tradition the builder has no sense of time or place other than his own, whereas the academic (or classical) tradition constantly makes reference to historical contexts. In parallel with the advance of academicism in architecture we have steadily lost our relationship with the indigenous tradition.[6] As a consequence the architect has been encouraged to search in history for the missing links in the chain of 'tradition', whilst the real tradition has been vanishing under his very eyes. This then is the architect's essential dilemma: he is trained to appreciate a series of unrelated historical abstractions whilst the present cries out for some response to its own indigenous patterns.

I believe that in rebelling against traditional technology and the formal solutions it imposes the student seeks these responses and must be encouraged and helped by every means. The student rebellion may be unpopular with established architects but this is simply because we have no clear ideas about responsibilities towards research and development within the profession as a *corpus*. It is nevertheless within this rebellion that the seeds of a future for architecture are being fertilized.

In search of order

Any attempt to clarify the architect's role (rather than his sense of professionalism) is confronted by the 'complexity conspiracy'. This usually takes the form of an outcry about systems and confusions in communications techniques, all of which are advanced as excuses for lowering standards of performance. Without the basic discipline of traditional skills the student is lost in the confusion of an architectural language which is not eloquent and a rhetoric which is not architecture. The case for inaction, that certain restrained indolence which characterizes various sectors of present British life, is also asserting itself in undergraduate attitudes in our schools of architecture. There is a new atmosphere of *ennui* which surrounds the curriculum: the student, who is in touch with wider social and human issues, questions the values and standards of a professional, quasi-Masonic indoctrination. Clearly, the argument goes, there is too much information available.[1] Thus, only a smattering can be acquired in any one field, a superficial glossary of terms which are only loosely linked. If we do not get through a syllabus in undergraduate work we can go on to postgraduate study. The academic programme can now be extended almost indefinitely and, as a consequence, decisions can be postponed. What is required is a real hard core of skills which could be acquired in the first three years, with a one or two year layer of experiment and speculation before going on to truly postgraduate research.

The sin of our immediate architectural forefathers, as judged now, is that they cared for appearances, about aesthetic matters at the expense of functional ones, or functional ones at the expense of economic ones, or economic ones at the expense of appearance; that above all they were concerned about their own appearances; that they were preoccupied with questions of territorial prerogative, with social and conference table hierarchies rather than management decisions. And management, as we now know, is more influential than anything else, even knowledge and skill! With management, after all, come the twin benefits of drama and ritual, whereas the acquisition of knowledge and skill may be only a routine affair. Not long ago architects cared about their role because they had taken a kind of Hippocratic oath to practise their profession in the interests of 'enriching' society and its way of life. Admittedly they were often ill-equipped but they devoted themselves to the task in good faith. Many were serious men, if often misled by passing fashions and handicapped by imperfect knowledge. At least they had goals and something that approached vision, even if this was blurred by the deterministic attitudes of such would-be prophets as Le Corbusier.

In 1963 Christian Norberg-Schultz[2] wrote: 'The present situation of architecture is confused and puzzling. From the client we hear constant complaints about the architect's lack of ability to satisfy him, from a practical as well as from an aesthetical and economical point of view. The authorities give us to understand that it is often doubtful whether the architects are qualified to solve the problems which society poses. And the architects themselves disagree on issues so fundamental that their discussion must be interpreted as groping uncertainty. The disagreement does not concern only the so-called "aesthetic" problems, but also the fundamental questions of how man should live and work in buildings and cities. It is also characteristic that architectural education has been under revision for a long time. New didactic principles are wanted, but the ends and the means are in dispute. All these symptoms unite to indicate a confusion in our environment which we do not agree about how to unravel. The unified character we know from cities and architectural lay-outs of the past is becoming a dying memory.' In 1920 in latter-day optimism after the holocaust W. R. Lethaby wrote: 'As the old Greek said, "The city teaches the man"'. So our stable societies gave us ordered cities, which in turn gave us ordered civilizations, until they decayed and fell to the Barbarians. Since we said goodbye to the stable society in the Western world, since the First World War, we have, to quote the title of C. P. Cavafy's poem, been 'Waiting for the Barbarians'. Not unnaturally, as we have been waiting for half a century, we are in the predicament described in the last three stanzas of that poem:

What does this sudden uneasiness mean,
And this confusion? (How grave the faces have become!)
Why are the streets and squares rapidly emptying,
And why is everyone going back home lost in thought?
Because it is night and the barbarians have not come.
And some men have arrived from the frontiers
And they say that barbarians don't exist any longer.
And now, what will become of us without barbarians?
They were a kind of solution.

Paul Klee maintained that it is the artist's purpose to create Cosmos (order) out of Chaos.[3] We know that this was the purpose of the temple builders in Classical Greece, who aided this process by developing clearly defined hierarchies of order, what we know as the Doric, Ionic and Corinthian Orders of architecture. But Klee expected to seek order from his own time by empirical rather than pragmatic principles.

Anton Ehrenzweig has many interesting observations on this aspect of the creative process. He wrote: 'The chaos of the unconscious is as deceptive as the chaos of outer reality. In either case we need the less differentiated techniques of unconscious vision to become aware of their hidden order. The scientist has to face the fragmentation of physical facts with courage. He has to scan a multitude of possible links that could make sense out of apparent chaos . . . The artist, too, has to face chaos in his work before unconscious scanning brings about the integration of his work as well as of his own personality. My point will be that unconscious scanning makes use of undifferentiated modes of vision that to normal awareness would seem chaotic. Hence comes the impression that the primary process merely produces chaotic fantasy material that has to be ordered and shaped by the ego's secondary processes. On the contrary, the primary process is a precision instrument for creative scanning that is far superior to discursive reason and logic.'[4]

Today we can no longer accept a dogmatic imposition of rules for aesthetic order in building, although it is perhaps ironic that our unwillingness to accept aesthetic rules has been paralleled by the advent of an ever-increasing number of building and planning regulations. Similarly, we cannot hope to combat social discontent in housing with arguments about principles of aesthetic order or the imposition of cultural values on those who do not have those values. The Roman Church could not achieve the counter-reformation it strove for because its clergy failed to understand that the problem was not one of 'a reformed church' (in the sense of it being an institution) but of reformed Man who, having freed himself from the shackles of imposed dogma, sought the existential experience of a personal revelation. He was no longer connected to the myth in the machine. This is also the dilemma of the architect today. Is it that architecture as we know it has always been, like the theatre, an essentially middle-class preoccupation? Perhaps the real consequence of the enlightenment and post-eighteenth-century revolutions is that we are free to seek a new order, one based on the exploration of human needs and the rational employment of natural resources. But in order to engage in planning as a participatory and anticipatory process we must remove priority areas of action from the political arena, which is easier said than done. Similarly, it is necessary to identify and accommodate the rituals of our society in terms which are not limited by the inhibitions of outmoded craft traditions. Expressing a more pessimistic view in his book *Le Hasard et la Necessité*, Jacques Monod has recently reminded us that we now also have the privilege of destroying all natural systems, the world itself, without waiting for the process of evolution. That possibility puts the significance of architectural form into its proper perspective. But that significance has always been a minority interest and we are not absolved from concern and involvement in a cause on the grounds that the majority of our fellow men find no purpose in that activity. Vision reinforced by optimism (i.e. the forward projection of 'faith') is the best antidote to despair.

On the other hand one of our main problems at the present may be our preoccupation with intellectual pursuits in isolation from social phenomena which generate them and which they affect, or hope to affect. Perhaps, as Christopher Cornford suggested recently, it is Plato who is one of the principal culprits, because he made distinctions between the functions of the reasoning mind and those of the senses. Cornford draws a parallel between the development of public education in Great Britain over the past hundred years and the death of handicraft activities, saying that we seem to have bought the Platonic package with all its divisiveness. We are experiencing the consequences now. The increasing dominance of machine-based technology and its management has left idle the hands and minds of those who do not share in the higher education cake, and it is not surprising that some of those hands and minds rebel to destroy what little order is left.

So today, our cities are inclined to teach us about chaos and disorder. Is it because our modern cities are a product of 'planning' or the lack of it? By planning we should mean the rationalization of resources, the anticipation of future needs. But the planning we witness seems mostly to be conducted from a number of disparate band-wagons, one for housing, one for road transport, etc., which go about like ambulances attempting, as Ian Fulton says, 'to patch up gaping wounds with bits of Elastoplast'. Small wonder that we are in need of 'new didactic principles'.

What is it that we are trying to achieve? Is it the shortest travelling time between two points, allowing the *ennui* to increase and multiply? Is it a new sense of community, a sense of unity similar to that which characterized the Roman Empire in the third and fourth centuries A.D.?[5] Or is it no longer possible to identify objectives? If that is the case, can we really plan or design at all?

Of course the increased density of population in the new industrial-urban *milieu* is relevant, as George Steiner suggests.[6] 'We conduct a good part of our lives amid the menacing jostle of the crowd. Enormous pressures of competing numbers build up against our needs of space, of privacy. The result is a contradictory impulse towards "clearance". On the one hand, the palpable mass of uniform life, the insect immensity of the city or the beach crowd, devalues any sense of individual worth. It wholly deflates the mystery of the irreplaceable presence [Steiner's term for God]. On the other hand, and because our own identity is threatened by the smothering mass of the anonymous, we suffer destructive spasms, a blind need to lunge out and make room. Elias Canetti has made the intriguing suggestion that the ease of the holocaust relates to the collapse of currency in the 1920s. Large numbers lost all but a vaguely sinister, unreal meaning. Having seen a hundred thousand, then a million, then a billion marks needed to buy bread or a bus ticket, ordinary men lost all perception of concrete enormity. The same large numbers tainted with unreality the disappearance and liquidation of peoples. There is evidence that men and women are only imperfectly adapted to co-exist in the stifling proximity of the industrial-urban hive. Accumulating over a century, the increase in noise levels, in the pace of work and motion, may have reached a pathological limit and triggered instincts of devastation.' And the computer, of course, has also speeded up the depersonalization process by the very pace and abstract nature of its operations. Our lives are increasingly dominated by machines and mechanization, but we ourselves are not machines. Le Corbusier's slogan that 'a house is a machine for living in' expresses not only a depersonalization but also a despiritualization of our society and values.

Again I quote from Steiner: 'The new façades, crowded, economically dynamic as may be the spaces behind them, speak a curious emptiness. The test case lies in the restored urban centres. At great pains and cost, *Altstädte*, whole cities, have been rebuilt, stone by numbered stone, geranium pot by geranium pot. Photographically there is no way of telling; the patina on the gables is even richer than before. But there is something unmistakably amiss. Go to Dresden or Warsaw, stand in one of the exquisitely recomposed squares in Verona, and you will feel it. The perfection of renewal has a lacquered depth. As if the light at the cornices had not been restored, as if the air were inappropriate and carried still an edge of fire. There is nothing mystical to this impression; it is almost painfully literal. It may be that the coherence of the ancient thing is harmonic with time, that a perspective of a street, of a roofline that have lived their natural being, can be replicated but not recreated (even where it is, ideally, indistinguishable from the original, reproduction is not the vital form). Handsome as it is, the Old City of Warsaw is a stage-set; walking through it, the living create no active resonance. It is the image of those precisely restored housefronts, of those managed lights and shadows which I keep in mind when trying to discriminate between what is irretrievable – though it may still be about – and what has in it the pressure of life.'

The reconstruction of the old city of Warsaw after destruction by the Germans was undertaken in the wake of the Communist *coup* in Poland. On the basis of Bellotto's panoramic paintings of the old quarter the decision was made to turn back the clock not merely to 1939 but to 1689 (Fig.11). It is an appeal made in totally bad faith to the natural romanticism of the Polish spirit. It is the machine weathering and wearing of the reconstructed buildings that is so nauseating. Everywhere one can taste the brickdust of a recently tooled piece of instant history. Therefore it has no active resonance, no pressure of life. We may not know exactly what architecture is but we know what it cannot be. It is no cover-up for political régimes or social omissions. Albert Speer could enshrine the Nazi spirit in his buildings, but his clean, sterile lines spoke mainly of the process of racial purification which could have no lasting echoes in the hearts of men.

The new Chancellery, Berlin
by Albert Speer (1938).

Enforced order is no alternative for natural order because it is merely *ersatz*. That which is dogmatic can no longer last. Our hope is in that which is revealed and worked out by an intensive personal search for knowledge. Our main task as designers is surely to assist this personal exploration at all levels of society so that form does not become an obstacle to understanding and identity. That makes our task infinitely more difficult than we have so far realized, requiring more relevant knowledge and experience than we have so far been able to harness. And our academic programme which divides practical buildings from theoretical speculation is at the root of our present failures to enmesh. The task is enormous and our educational facilities hopelessly inadequate: it is therefore primarily a test for the will and the imagination. In our dilemma we could choose between (1) classical order (for which we no longer have a basis), (2) anonymous indigenousness (which we no longer comprehend) or (3) the romantic (which being sensuous rather than cerebral is no longer respectable). If our academic *ennui* is not cured we are in danger of dissipating our energies in self-abuse, neglecting the wider horizons of needs and resources which we might describe as the new erogenous zones.

The city and the politics of form

As a Greek, Cavafy was immersed in Plato's concept of blood and soil, and most of his poetry is a commentary on the conflicts and ambiguities of political institutions, e.g. the City State.

His concern in the poem *In a Large Greek Colony, 200* BC[1] is the problem of introducing a political reformer. There are objections, he says, because these reformers make an enormous fuss and radical reforms enter their heads, which demand to be executed without delay. He points out that they also have a liking for sacrifice, that they have a tendency to condemn ownership when this suits them and he goes on:

And when, with luck, the business is completed,
and every detail is defined and circumscribed,
they retire, taking also the wages due to them,
allowing us to see whatever still remains, after
such effective surgery.

Cavafy concludes with the stanza:

Perhaps the moment has not yet arrived.
Let us not hurry: speed is a dangerous thing.
Untimely measures bring repentance.
Certainly, and unhappily, many things are wrong in the Colony.
But is there anything human without imperfection?
And after all, look, we do go forward.

A hundred-and-fifty years before, in the age of enlightenment, at the close of a century dedicated to a realization of human perfection and on the eve of the French Revolution, William Godwin had a more *optimistic* view.[2] '. . . man is perfectible, or, in other words, susceptible to perpetual improvement. Once establish the perfectibility of man, and it will inevitably follow that we are advancing to a state, in which truth will be too well known to be easily mistaken, and justice too habitually practised to be voluntarily counteracted.'

Godwin's belief that knowledge, science, wealth, social organization and moral behaviour – even Man himself – are indefinitely improvable represents a high point in the literature of progress. He remained unshaken by the processes of the French Revolution, which began in the same year as the first edition of *Political Justice*, and the editions of 1796 and 1798 were unaltered. He believed that reason would prevail and that the more knowledge we have the more moral we shall be and the more able, therefore, to work out with certainty and precision the preconditions for our own happiness. Godwin's position was attacked by Malthus in his *Essay on Population*, who warned that material improvement would be accompanied by an increased population, outgrowing food production and restoring poverty and misery. But Godwin's faith in reason prevailed and, in the second edition of his essay, Malthus conceded that a wiser population would voluntarily and painlessly restrain its increase.

Godwin's book was eagerly seized upon by a large section of the middle classes, who were anxious for some reassurance on their own moral position although its only formula for progress was a blending of liberty, anarchy and education, with Government seen as an unnecessary evil in an enlightened society. In spite of its considerable sales its social and political influence was small.

Godwin's contemporary, John Millar, expressed a conflicting view in his theory of *Moral Sentiments*, published at the beginning of the nineteenth century. 'In an age where there is little industry, or desire of accumulation, neighbouring and dependent societies are apt to rob and plunder each other; but the members of the same society are attracted by a common interest, and are often strongly united in the bonds of friendship and affection, by mutual exertions of benevolence, or by accidental habits of sympathy. But in a country where nobody is idle, and where every person is eager to augment his fortune, or to improve his circumstances, there occur innumerable competitions and rivalships, which contract the heart and set mankind at variance. In proportion as every man is attentive to his own advancement, he is vexed and tormented by every obstacle to his prosperity, and prompted to regard his competitors with envy, resentment and other malignant passions. That there is no friendship in trade is an established maxim among traders. Every man for himself and God Almighty for us all, is their fundamental doctrine.'[3]

Nevertheless, eighteenth-century life and developments in Edinburgh, 'the Athens of the North,' had clearly demonstrated that commercial advancement and morality were inseparable allies in the modern city and this allowed Adam Smith in his *Wealth of Nations* to speak against the idea that *laissez-faire* capitalism was altogether the enemy of moral improvement and human progress:[4]

' . . . every individual . . . neither intends to promote the public interest, nor knows how much he is promoting it . . . by directing industry in such a manner as its produce may be of the greatest value, he intends only his own gain, and he is in this, as in many other cases, led by an invisible hand to promote an end which has no part of his intention.

'Nor is it always the worse for the society that it should be no part of it. By pursuing his own interest he frequently promotes that of the society more effectually than when he really intends to promote it. I have never known much good done by those who affected to trade for the public good.'

Indeed, argues Smith, accumulation of wealth brings with it an increased standard of living for all, in other words a redistribution of wealth to the attendant population:

'the rich . . . are led by an invisible hand to make nearly the same distribution of the necessities of life which would have been made had the earth been divided into equal proportions among all its inhabitants, and thus, without intending it, without knowing it, advance the interests of society: and afford means to the multiplication of the species . . .'

This led him to the conclusion that the poor were:

'In what constitutes the real happiness of human life . . . in no respect inferior to those who would seem so much above them.'

If we were to adopt the historicist's approach, it is clear that we would have plenty of evidence to suggest that political and economic theory as presented by different exponents in different ages '. . . is a tale told by an idiot, full of sound and fury, signifying nothing'.

The source of all theory of political institutions is, of course, Plato's *Republic*. And Plato tells us: 'It is the business of the rulers of the city, if it is anybody's, to tell lies, deceiving both its enemies and its own citizens for the benefit of the city; and no one else must touch this privilege.'

It is important to understand Plato's concept of the ruler of the State, the Government in other words, as 'a doctor who is not afraid to administer strong medicines'. As Crossman points out, the deceits or strong medicine that Plato has in mind mean: 'propaganda, the technique of controlling the behaviour of . . . the bulk of the ruled majority'. And Popper argues that it is Plato's intention not to reserve 'the lies' for the consumption of the 'ruled' alone, with the rulers themselves a fully enlightened intelligentsia, but: '. . . the rulers themselves should believe in the propaganda . . . increasing its wholesome effect, i.e. of strengthening the rule of the master race, and, ultimately, of arresting all political change'.[5]

Plato understood the impact of *all* influences on the senses and his view of education provided for the censoring of these stimuli so that only 'good influences' imprinted themselves on the soul. The problem of all forms of censorship centres on the question: 'what is good and for whom?' In our open-ended society, as Marshall McLuhan has suggested,[6] the whole propaganda machine *is* a totally permeating system which reflects the interests of both the ruled and the rulers:

'Cities were always a means of achieving some degree of simultaneity of association and awareness among men. What the family and the tribe had done in this respect for a few, the city did for many. Our technology now removes all city walls and pretexts. The oral and acoustic space of tribal cultures had never met visual reconstruction of the past. All experience and all past lives were *now*. Preliterate man knew only simultaneity. The walls between men, and between arts and sciences, were built on the written or visually arrested word.

'With the return to simultaneity we enter the tribal and acoustic world once more. Globally.'

Nevertheless 'the lies' remain. Those who control the media become the new liars and all the pretexts are not, therefore, removed. In fact the multiplicity of media serve to distort both the problem and the solution. And whereas the walls between men have been taken down in this electronic age, it is the ruled who suffer more from the resultant lack of privacy than the rulers.

The rich do not distribute their wealth as Adam Smith imagined and it is still money that buys privacy. Chermayeff and Alexander have underlined this. 'Privacy is most urgently needed and most critical in the place where people live . . . the dwelling is the little environment into which all the stresses and strains of the large world are today intruding, in one way or another, ever more deeply.'

McLuhan makes the error of identifying the immediacy of the electronic communications systems with a single simplistic environment, i.e. 'the electronic village', and Sir Peter Medawar has pinpointed this kind of error. 'Although we cheerfully speak about *the* environment of an organism or a population, we know well there is no such thing. A population of individuals lives in a range of environments, narrow or wide as the case may be; and adaptability is just as much a matter of being adapted to environments which differ from place to place as to environments which change from time to time.'

Chermayeff and Alexander outline some of the problems of failing to respond to the totally propaganda-polluted environment that McLuhan describes:

'A new physical urban order is needed to give expression and meaning to the life of "urbanising man", to clarify, to define, to give integrity to human purposes and organisation, and finally, to give these *form*.

'Today modern cities and other man-made elements in the physical environment are becoming shapeless for lack of an informing principle. But no such principle will be forthcoming, and no action will be taken, until the processes of design are themselves informed and controlled by the recognition of new realities.

'While failing to produce satisfactory new environments we are losing the best of the old . . . unique and irreplaceable places, buildings, many memorials, and entire historic cities, man's most telling evidence of a communal way of life – are being neglected or totally destroyed . . . the statue of Eros, once the delight of strolling visitors to Piccadilly Circus, has become unreachable.'

It will be noted that their manifesto is pivoted on two concerns: (1) that the informing principle of planning must in turn be informed and controlled by the 'recognition of new realities'; and (2) a straightforward romantic view on the conservation of existing urban structures and their 'significance'.

All the conflicts of principle and action reviewed above come into focus, for example, in the proposals for the redevelopment of Covent Garden in London (Fig.12). Here is one of the most complex bits of London's urban infrastructure located only half a mile from Eros, with that juxtaposition of places of work, entertainment and residence that cuts across all boundaries of class, occupation and exclusiveness, yet the underprivileged residents and small shopkeepers are being priced out in the name of a utopian planning proposal which purports to be based on a thorough social-science survey of residents' needs and desires. The Greater London Council's planner in charge of the Covent Garden proposals has said that in the matter of obtaining accurate, unbiased, and usable information on needs and desires the planner was entirely in the hands of the social survey team. But whatever credibility we may wish to extend to the team's results, as incorporated in the proposals, has largely been demolished by the statements of the underprivileged residents of 'the Garden', who have no desire to be displaced but whose request for replacement accommodation at a rental they can afford has not been met by the plan.[9] This does not, of course, make one optimistic about the success of so-called participation in the planning process.

This is perhaps another example of Plato's 'lies', because the evidence collected by the social survey team was 'synthesized' to produce an *ersatz* for needs and desires which reflects the interests of the 'rulers' – in this case an amalgam of politicians and developers – rather than a reflection of the actual needs and desires of the present residents or the supposed idealism of the planners.

Let us return to Plato, or rather to Sir Karl Popper's view of Plato's political theory, as outlined in the first volume of *The Open Society and its Enemies*:

'Inherent in Plato's programme there is a certain approach towards politics which, I believe, is most dangerous. Its analysis is of great practical importance from the point of view of rational social engineering. The Platonic approach I have in mind can be described as that of Utopian engineering, as opposed to another kind of social engineering which I consider as the only rational one, and which may be described by the name of piecemeal engineering. The Utopian approach is the more dangerous as it may seem to be the obvious alternative to an out-and-out historicism – to a radically historicist approach which implies that we cannot alter the course of history; at the same time, it appears to be a necessary complement to a less radical historicism, like that of Plato, which permits human interference.

'The Utopian approach may be described as follows. Any rational action must have a certain aim. It is rational in the same degree as it pursues its aim consciously and consistently, and as it determines its means according to this end. To choose the end is therefore the first thing we have to do if we wish to act rationally; and we must be careful to determine our real or ultimate ends, from which we must distinguish those intermediate or partial ends, which actually are only means, or steps on the way, to the ultimate end.'

'Civilised individuals hate and resent the civilisation that makes their lives possible. What they love is an imaginary human situation invented by their own genius and which they believe is the only true and human reality.' So says Herzog in Saul Bellow's novel of that name, suggesting that for this reason the concept of Utopia of which Thomas More wrote in 1516 is, from the existential point of view, an attitude in 'bad faith'.

In his *Utopia* More describes the pattern of urban life in 'no-place', for that is the real meaning of Utopia. 'Each town consists of 6000 households, not counting the county ones, and to keep the population fairly steady there's a law that no household shall contain less than ten or more than 16 adults. This law is observed by simply moving supernumerary adults to smaller households. If a town gets too full the surplus population is transferred to a town that's comparatively empty . . . Every town is divided into four districts of equal size, each with its own shopping centre in the middle of it. There the products of every household are collected in warehouses, and then distributed according to type among various shops. When the head of a household needs anything for himself or his family, he just goes to one of these shops and asks for it. And he's allowed to take it away without any sort of payment either in money or kind. There's more than enough to go round, and why should anyone want to start hoarding when he knows he'll never have to go short of anything? . . . These shopping centres include provision markets, to which they take meat and fish, as well as bread, fruit and vegetables. But there are special places outside the town where all blood and dirt are first washed off in running water. The slaughtering of livestock and the cleaning of carcasses is done by slaves. They don't let ordinary people get used to cutting up animals, because they think it tends to destroy one's natural feelings of humanity. It's also forbidden to bury anything dirty or unhygienic inside the town, for fear of polluting the atmosphere and causing disease.'

So, More's ideal city has certain prerequisites:
(1) fixed population,
(2) fixed production, by householders,
(3) slaves to perform the unhygienic tasks and emotionally distressing jobs,
(4) totalitarian government to enforce these principles.

It will be useful to bear these precepts in mind when we study what has actually happened in the history of urban communities since classical times, especially in the Middle Ages and the Renaissance, because these two periods, if one can really separate them on the evidence that has been left us, represent the maximum contrast of formal attitude and formal solution. In More's *Utopia* there is production but no trade, the late Roman and Carolingian cities had trade but no production, the ideal cities of the Renaissance catered more for garrisons (also subject to regulation) rather than communities. Yet we continue to strive for this formal perfection as did Ledoux, Garnier and Le Corbusier. Are we all merely victims of the Utopian heresy? Is it perhaps the essence of our survival-potential that we hope one day to remove all the counter weights to environmental balance, that we imagine it is possible to live without the distresses of commerce, pollution, over-crowding and shortage of supplies. Do we, with Herzog, see how difficult it is to eradicate the notion of crises from our minds, do we unconsciously long for some one event that will change things irrevocably and tell us how, from then on, we are to lead our lives? Is it our sense of Paradise, from the Persian *faradis* meaning garden, that makes us grasp after Eden, the physical and material perfection before the Fall? The renewal of urbanization in tenth- and eleventh-century Western Europe is perhaps best understood if it is compared with similar developments that characterized Roman civilization from the sixth century B.C. until its climax in the imperial period. Urbanization depends upon industrialization, i.e. an organized process of production, and the Romans had a genius for order and organization which they made the basis of the Roman state and culture. But a workable and durable urban civilization has as its prerequisite a social and political system in which human passions and economic pressures are held more or less in balance. The Romans had no panacea for this conflict of passions and economics, a problem that is rooted in all highly developed societies. The masses were mollified by bread, circuses and army careers; while the theatre, the baths, the prospect of a good position in the civil service and a comfortable retirement in the country met the ambitions of the middle and upper classes. The hopeless had to make do with the succour of mystery religions until the State recognition of Christianity in 313. But it was not the advent of Christianity that heralded the decline of the Roman Empire so much as the gradual throttling of Mediterranean trade which began in the seventh century with the advance of Islam.

The Carolingian Empire inherited the Roman urban fabric at the beginning of the ninth century, and the ancient cities were used as places of habitation and fortified settlements from which the surrounding countryside could be controlled. But the Carolingian administrative, legal and economic reforms were not so much anti-urban or anti-expansionist; rather Carolingian ideals as expressed in art and architecture represented a vision of reconstituted ancient grandeur. Bishops and clergy contented themselves on the whole with repairing walls where necessary and building the occasional fort and cathedral. Merchants' settlements, mainly outside the city walls, were small and dwindling. Production and trade shrank to a minimum. Towns were no longer centres of manufacture and exchange, they had become essentially places of consumption. The gradual decline of the Roman Empire had its roots in this swing to consumption in the Italian cities as production moved to the East and to Western Europe. Transportation of agricultural and manufactured goods became more risky, mostly as a consequence of the activities of Muslim and Teutonic tribes and Norsemen, and this led in turn to increasing stagnation of urban society in the West as well.

Carolingian society centred rather on the monastery, as is indicated by the celebrated plan of St Gall which is based on the Forum of Trajan in its formal relationships. Cloister, chapter hall, church, and laboratoria derive directly from the great colonnaded square, the basilica, the temple and markets of its Roman model, yet all the marks of a true city are absent. True some of the monastic production was for the market but trading was carried on in remote markets on a commission basis. Exchange between the members of the community was non-existent, trade with those who passed through only minimal. It cannot even be argued that the monastic scheme embodied in the St Gall manuscript and manifested in numerous abbeys from the ninth century onwards retained the elements of the city in capsule form until the time when the prerequisites for an urban revival were again in evidence. The monasteries were mostly isolated in the country, away from major trade routes, and played but little part in the rebirth of urban culture, while few of them formed the basis of significant new cities. For this reason the St Gall plan would appear as merely an exercise in formalism, and mediaeval cities, with the exception of the Bastide towns, while not totally unlike or uninfluenced by the classical tradition, evolved their own form and structure under very different social, political and economic conditions. The formal symmetries derived from the Hellenistic-Roman city and preserved in the plan of St Gall were not

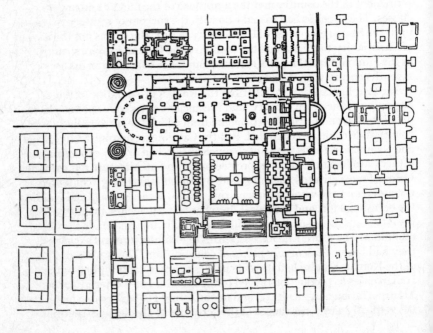

echoed in urban design until the advent of the Italian Renaissance in the quattrocento. Social and political evolution coupled with mercantile expansion is usually well ahead of the urban developments which make up their architectural and cultural framework. This was certainly the case in the eleventh and twelfth centuries, and by the time mediaeval cities had begun to attain their ultimate form new social, political, and cultural forces were converting the high noon of the Middle Ages to twilight. It is, of course, difficult to examine the mediaeval city in its pure state. The urban fabric was, throughout the tenth to the fifteenth centuries, in a constant state of metamorphosis, and the student of mediaeval cities has none of the virgin records which await the student of mediaeval politics or economics. The *Altstadt* boasting a secular building dating from before the fifteenth century is rare indeed. Cities like Dinkelsbühl and Rothenburg, museum towns, have little of the pre-fifteenth century within their walls. As Saalman says:[10] 'It is the Renaissance butterfly we are looking at, not the Mediaeval caterpillar.' When one is tempted to speak of the perfection in the mediaeval city, as if there were one perfect finite statement of the Middle Ages that expressed itself with equal clarity in urban form, one must recall the lack of evidence. Detailed topographical analysis of cities did not begin until the late sixteenth and early seventeenth centuries, in the hands of Braun and Hogenberg, Merian and Hollar, and as evidence of the mediaeval city is only partial. Urban patterns, however, once established undergo very slow mutation, and many of the original features remained in some form at least until the last century. What is important to understand about the mediaeval city is that it was an organic thing, living on its heritage and building upon it, with constant modifications, especially on its periphery.

Vitruvius outlined the fundamental considerations to be observed in the design of towns in Book I chapters IV to VII of *De Architectura* and he describes, as an example of an ideal city, the essential elements of a town with a circular plan form, viz. I VI 6–7: 'In the middle of the city place a marble *amussium* . . . then, opening your compasses to this point which marks the length of the gnomon's shadow, describe a circle from the centre . . . the rest of the entire circumference is then to be divided into three equal parts on each side, and thus we have designed a figure equally apportioned among the eight winds. Then let the directions of your streets and alleys be laid down on the lines of division between the quarters of the two winds.' In chapter V he sets out the principles of wall construction and the position and shape of towers, speaking against the square tower on the grounds of its weakness in attack on its quoins. Otherwise his principles remained good until 1453, when the fall of Constantinople to the Turks marked the beginning of a new era of military engineering.

Basically the mediaeval builders followed Vitruvius's prescription for the walls, gates and towers around their irregular plan forms (Fig.13). They were, of course, not merely for defence in time of war but for control of entry and exit in peacetime. For this reason the gates remained the critical features. Not only did one pass in and out by the gate, it was also a place where one waited, waiting for the guards to check one's goods, to pay one's toll, and, waiting, chatted, drank, and slept. The outside of the gate therefore assumed an importance of its own; inns were built there and the seeds of new extra-mural communities were sown. A *faubourg*, a false town, was thus established, a parasite attaching itself to one of the city's lifelines. Now, the walls of mediaeval city were subject to an unwritten law, that for economic reasons they should invariably follow the smallest possible perimeter. The *bourgeois* with his house, shop and church within the walls had no interest in enlarging those walls. It must be for those who had been left outside the original walls to pay for their emendation. As Saalman says: 'The story of mediaeval cities is of people trying to get into town, not out of it.' In the town the feudal structure of baron, soldier and serf was largely broken down by the fact that existence was based on the production and exchange of goods and services, in other words, supply and demand; one lived in the city in order to utilize its facilities – markets, access roads, delivery carts, fresh water, notaries, town officials, churches, all necessary for transactions based on oath and other business.

The worst possible place to be located in business was on the perimeter wall between two gates, i.e. away from the arterial roads that connected the gates with the city centre, which meant in turn that one would be farthest from the centre and linked with it only by indirect route. These factors explain why settlements tended to have a starfish structure rather than being laid out in concentric rings. So, little pockets of undesirable ground were left unsettled within the walls, while at the gates the *faubourgs* were prospering. Often the *faubourg* markets were larger than those within the walls, and they had the advantage of avoiding or evading city taxes. This last consideration must have weighed heavily with the *bourgeoisie* in their decision to include the *faubourgs* within the walls. Whatever the advantages of economic competition gained by remaining outside the city, the protection, services, legal privileges and real market opportunities were a clear case for going inside the wall.

Often mediaeval cities straddled the two banks of a river, i.e. a bridgehead was separated from the city walls by a strong gate – Rheims and Trier were examples of this form – but the land on the other side of the bridgehead was developed as a *faubourg*, Southwark's relationship to London being one example of this kind of development, and Frankfurt and Sachsenhausen being another (Fig.14).

Certainly mediaeval cities did not achieve the symmetrical perfection recommended by Virtruvius and it is interesting to note that his prescription was a marriage of topography and other environmental factors. But Roman organization did not allow for the free play of economic forces. It was not until the advent of new autocratic empires in the wake of the Italian Renaissance that determinism came into its own again. For example the Spanish kings required their *conquistadores* to lay out colonial towns on a grid-iron pattern with a large square dominating the centre and surrounded by the church and other principal buildings. Risks about the success or failure of such a pre-determined form could only be taken by a centrally administered national State with a vast scale of human and material resources to hand. This factor probably accounts for the relatively small number of projected ideal cities that were actually built. Nevertheless, the Renaissance, with the rediscovery of Vitruvius, sparked off tremendous interest in finding ideal solutions to the problems of urban living, solutions that were based, however, on theoretical premises rather than the economic dynamism that had generated the great mediaeval towns. As we have already seen in the case of the Carolingians, the idea alone is not enough. But as a preface to the idealization of urban patterns in our own time and as an exercise in rational geometry the ideal city projections of the Renaissance have a value all of their own, an abstract value rather than a utilitarian one, except in the purely military sense.

The ultimate source of all post-quattrocento architectural theory was Vitruvius's *De Architectura*, and after Alberti's *De re aedificatoria* it was the fountainhead of all Renaissance architectural writings. Cesare Cesariano prepared the first translation into Italian and, with magnificent illustrations, it appeared in Como in 1521; this was followed by Francesco Lucio's from Castel Durants (Venice, 1524), G. B. Caporali (Perugia, 1526) and most importantly that of Daniel Barbaro, patriach of Aquileia (Venice, 1556).

Alberti's work was written in Rome between 1443–52 with the specific purpose of engendering the rebirth of the ancient city, but Antonio Filarete's treatise, written between 1451 and 1464 in Milan, expressed a more direct interest in city planning. It was conceived as a series of *conversazione* between the architect and his *signore*, Francesco Sforza (1401–66), and contains a detailed description of an ideal city, Sforzinda – an octagonal star, with a carefully drawn distinction between the areas of administration and those of production and exchange. Francesco di Georgio Martini wrote in 1482, at the court of Urbino, a treatise which gave various plans for cities, devoting special attention to the relation between the internal arrangement and the fortified city wall; Vignola's *Regole*, published in 1562, sets the scene for standardization in architecture, reducing architecture to second place in relation to the overall unity and monumentality of the city plan.

The fifth book of Martini's *Trattato di Architettura* is regarded by some authorities as the true beginning of the new science of military engineering. This is disputed by Blomfield, who gives the credit to Michele san Michele of Verona, calling him the true forerunner of the great French engineer Vauban. Nevertheless Martini was the most prolific designer of ideal cities, catering for a wide variety of site conditions, including a centralized city adapted to hilltop conditions.

Pietro Cataneo's *Quattro Libri di Architettura* appeared in Venice in 1554 and included a number of plans based on the regular polygon with a separate citadel for the city's ruler, which doubtless influenced the plan of Mannheim founded in 1606.

1592 saw the publication, also in Venice, of Buonainto Lorini's *Fortificazione Libri Cinque*, and showed how the defence zones in front of the walls was increasing in size in an attempt to keep the attackers well away from the city. Vincenzo Scamozzi is however the only theorist credited with the realization of an ideal city. Although authorship of the plan for Palma Nova is in dispute he is credited with its construction, begun in 1593. In 1615 he published at Venice his *L'idea della Architettura Universale* which contains a plan similar to Palma Nova but with a grid-iron plan replacing the radial street pattern. Francesco de Marelli insisted on the defensive effectiveness of the scissors plan in his *Dell Architettura militare* (Brescia, 1599), which intensified the plasticity of the city's external form.

Twenty years after Vignola's *Regole* appeared, Fontana planned the reform of Rome, stripping buildings of their individuality, reducing the whole city to a street plan, and applying classical forms as merely symbolic stigmata of the urban scene.

City perimeters continued to be marked by walls, indicating an isolation from surrounding territory: these defences also affected the character of architecture within the walls. Renaissance treatises on architecture usually fall into two categories – those dealing with military architecture on the one hand, and civic architecture on the other. Architects worked in both spheres and even a pure Platonist like Michelangelo was versed in the essentials of fortifications. We might emphasize that during the Renaissance fortifications had both a defensive and offensive purpose; also military strategies and actions had been modified by the rapid developments in firearms and the way they were used. Battles were now conducted across open ground – no-man's land – so that a fortification had not only to resist bombardment but also to allow defenders to rake the surrounding area with cross fire. The perimeter of the ideal city, normally a many-pointed star form, stemmed directly from the geometry of necessity. To the problems of covering open ground were added those of dominating the areas immediately below the walls and of constructing those very walls so that they lessened the impact of projectiles, hence the complex form coupled with the steeply sloping surfaces. Battlements and towers were natural targets and gave way to low walls which made ready emplacements for heavy batteries. To the walls were added a complex pattern of projecting ramparts, outworks, moats and *glacis*, the whole system becoming so specialized a science and technology that it gave birth to a new profession, that of military engineering.

So the end of the sixteenth century finally saw the building of ideal cities, of which Palma Nova is one, whose only function was to accommodate military garrisons on vulnerable frontiers. Palma is a nine-sided polygon with its central square a regular hexagon. These forms are resolved and integrated into a complex pattern of radial streets, six

main ones and twelve subsidiaries leading from an inner concentric ring,
six of which cross secondary squares: the main public buildings are around
the central square. This type of military city clearly displayed the physical
forms of the Utopian ideal. They were merely instruments of society with
no true society of their own: as a consequence they were not subject to the
conflict of forces and objectives that characterise the evolution of urban
form in a non-idealistic society. It is curious therefore that Le Corbusier's
crie de cœur in the foreword to his book *Urbanisme* (1924) harks back to
Utopian ideals once more:

'A Town is a tool.
Towns no longer fulfil this function. They are ineffectual; they use up
our bodies, they thwart our souls.
The lack of order to be found everywhere in them offends us, their
degradation wounds our self-esteem and humiliates our sense of dignity.
They are not worthy of the age; they are no longer worthy of us.
A city!
It is the grip of man upon nature. It is a human operation directed
against nature, a human organism both for protection and for work. It is
a creation.
Geometry is the means, created by ourselves, whereby we perceive the
external world and express the world within us.
Geometry is the foundation.
It is also the material basis on which we build those symbols which
represent to us perfection and the divine.
It brings with it the noble joys of mathematics.
Machinery is the result of geometry. The age in which we live is therefore
essentially a geometrical one; all its ideas are orientated in the direction
of geometry: Modern art and thought – after a century of analysis – are
now seeking beyond what is merely accidental; geometry leads them to
mathematical forms, a more and more generalised attitude.'

   Although the *bourgeoisie* of the Middle Ages would have agreed with
Le Corbusier's first premise, history is not on his side as far as the
geometrical *Gestalt* is concerned.

Significant form in architecture

Recently a student asked when I would begin giving useful and practical tips. He had clearly missed the point of a course which was hopefully concerned with the philosophy of creativity. I had to remind him that a preoccupation with the practical could so easily put the horizon out of focus and seriously impair speculative thought which might in the long run prove more valuable than immediately useful and often ephemeral information. Any philosophy of education for architects must surely include the strategic speculative as well as the practical tactical. The pursuit of either to the exclusion of the other will leave us stranded in the mud of no-man's land. It is one of the anomalies of progress that often the surfeit of information strangles our speculative potential and causes it to atrophy. This tendency to be overcome by facts and their projected implications, to be reduced to a state of impotency by economic appraisals and statistical forecasts, has made nonsense of our economic and town-planning policies, and has contributed in turn to the architect's present dilemma. It is the cultivation of 'design' skills, his powers of abstract and lateral thinking, that will help him out of his present fix. At least it is agreed that the designer needs freedom of movement between the managerial and executive areas of environmental design: in this way he can develop for himself a truly entrepreneurial role. Management alone is not enough: it has been singularly lacking in a philosophy of resources – hence our present environmental crisis – nor is it endowed with the mathematical precision of actuarial science. The architect who acts as the mere executant is abused by both management and consumer for his trouble.

Having discussed some of the broad issues of design and design education, the *Gestalt* of architecture,[1] I want now to look at building form and the use of form made by society in its efforts to match form with ritual. There seems little point in discussing attempts at non-correlation, although those seeking example would do well to examine the plan of Liverpool's Metropolitan Cathedral where the forms are consistently

47

irrelevant to the structural realization of the third dimension.[2]

Worringer in his *Empathie und Abstraktion* (1908) concludes that: 'Any deeper enquiry into the nature of our scientific aesthetics must lead to the realisation that, measured against actual works of art, its applicability is extremely limited. This situation has long been evident in practice through the undisguised mutual antipathy that divides art historians and aestheticians. The objective science of art, and aesthetics, are now and will remain in the future incompatible disciplines. Confronted by the choice of abandoning the greater part of his material and contenting himself with a history of art criticism *ad usum aesthetici*, or forgoing all the lofty flights of aesthetics, the art historian naturally opts for the latter, and the two disciplines, so closely related in their subject-matter, continue to pursue parallel paths devoid of any contact. Perhaps the sole cause of this misunderstanding is the superstitious belief in the verbal concept 'art'. Caught up in this superstition, we again and again become entangled in the positively criminal endeavour to reduce the multiple significance of the phenomena to a single, unequivocable concept. We cannot shake ourselves free of this superstition. We remain the slaves of words, the slaves of concepts.'

If this is true of the historian's and critic's position, where does the practitioner stand today when it comes to the use of architectural language, i.e. the form and detail with which he endeavours to achieve a style response to the stimuli of ritual? Is it not yet another aspect of the architect's present dilemma that we live in an age where arbitrariness is the rule of the day? In other words, one cannot have significant form without significant functions: there is no legitimate style without a clearly identifiable ritual. The essence of the beaux-arts system was to teach the student that within the vocabulary of classical architectural language lay the complete range of forms and details with which he could answer any building problem. But it was the Roman architectural vocabulary, based on seventeenth- and eighteenth-century archaeological exploration, that formed the basis of the beaux-arts design language, the Roman style which combined the trabeated with the arcuated, the rectilinear shell with the dome. In that sense the source of our tradition in architectural education was a half-way house between what Read calls the 'lapidary art' of Greece and the Romanesque 'sensibility for space'. At the same time, because the new architecture generated by the Industrial Revolution passed into the hands of engineers, who responded more immediately to the functional demands of new building types, architects were cut off from the craft tradition that had lingered on since the mediaeval period and inherited instead the *ersatz* of the classical and Neoclassical forms. From this point of view the renaissance of interest in classical antiquity which began with the quattrocento can be seen as an interruption of a tradition which had its origins in the Romanesque period and continued until the sixteenth century, an interruption which contributed substantially to the schism between engineering and architecture and consequently to the death of a unified system that linked structural techniques with building design.

We often make the error of assuming that this schism is essentially a Western phenomenon: that in the East the bond between the craftsman and the designer has been miraculously maintained. Some light was thrown on this assumption by a Japanese architect, who was recently a guest lecturer at the Liverpool School. He asked which aspects of Japanese architecture would be of particular interest to students and it was suggested that he might speak to us about tea-houses and gardens. He smiled and shook his head: 'I do not know about tea-houses and gardens', he explained. 'You see, the gardens, they are made by gardeners, who arrange their plants and materials in accordance with traditional patterns. And the tea-houses are made by our carpenters, who will merely ask the client whether he wants a tea-house to be of this or that number of tatami.'

Clearly, our Japanese visitor knew something about tea-houses and gardens, but he regarded the design (or arrangement) of these elements as part of a specialized tradition. He spoke to us instead about 'the philosophy of design procedures' in Japan, and it was most revealing to discover that, apart from an overlay of Japanese symbolic terminology, they were an almost exact replica of our own and seemed to owe nothing to what we think of as traditional Japanese ritual and style.

This means that in Japan it is the gardener and the carpenter who have inherited the basic 'geometry of the environment',[3] and the architect's role becomes that of 'manager' or catalyst. My concern from this point on will be with the significant rather than the arbitrary geometry of environment, to make a case for recapturing that area of exploratory draughtsmanship that has largely passed to the engineer. It is the geometric description of space that allows it to be understood and manipulated and we now have the computer to simplify our task.

One course of regularity is the setting out of columns, the gridding required by the trabeated system to ensure that beams span on to their supports. This *Gestalt* generates the expressive form of the third dimension directly from the structural system, as in the Great Temple at Karnak for example: the system in accommodating the ritual delineates the style. But the system, the form, is not the style: that which is classical in basic form – for example because it is trabeated – is only classical in style if that basic form is developed by appropriate detail. This explains the difference between the Neoclassical work of Schinkel and German Fascist architecture of the 1930s, although the two may be said to have certain basic resemblances in form (Fig.16). To produce a classical temple on the Roman pattern, or rather to reproduce one, it would not be enough merely to follow the planning proportions prescribed by Vitruvius in Book IV, Chapter IV, 1: i.e. 'The length of a temple is adjusted so that its width may be half its length, and the actual cella one fourth greater in length than width, including the wall in which the folding doors are placed. Let the remaining three parts, constituting the pronaos, extend to the antae terminating walls, which antae ought to be the same thickness as the

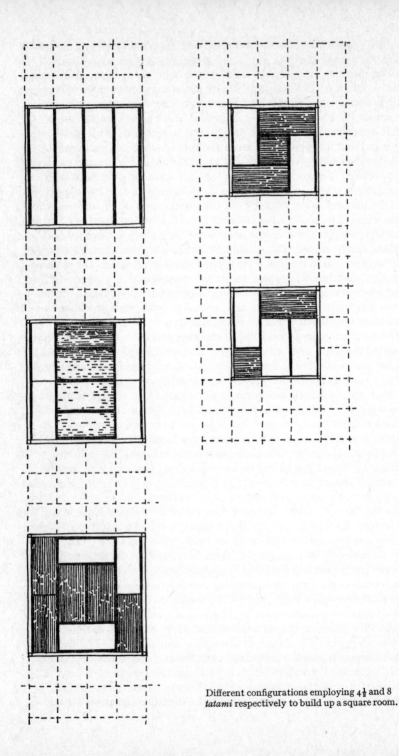

Different configurations employing 4½ and 8 *tatami* respectively to build up a square room.

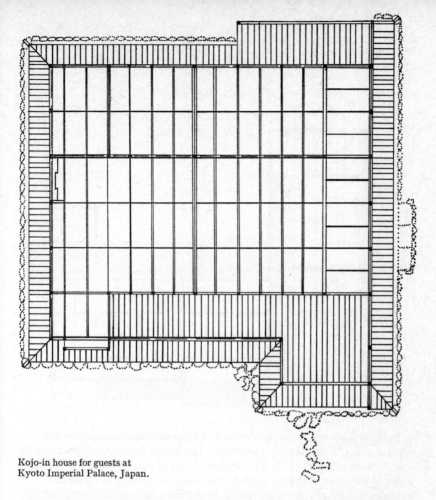

Kojo-in house for guests at
Kyoto Imperial Palace, Japan.

columns. If the temple is more than 20 ft in width, let the two columns be
placed between the antae, to separate the pteroma from the pronaos. The
three intercolumniations between the antae and the columns should be
closed by low walls made of marble or of joiner's work, with doors in them
to afford passages into the pronaos.'

Vitruvius goes on to discuss the proportions of the columns and the
details, but the whole logic of his prescription, even the proportions of the
plan which is two squares, is an abstraction, a copyist's formula which has
no apparent connexion with the original ritual. The *Gestalt* is missing.
It was such formulae that undermined the architect's function and
impoverished the true nature of architecture.

Let us contrast this academic tradition, as transcribed by the Beaux-
Arts schools, with traditional forms in Japanese architecture, again taking
the square as the significant or generative form.

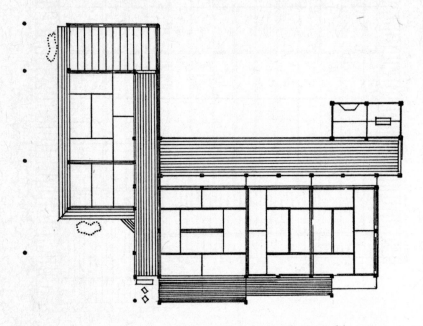

In the traditional Japanese house and tea-house the *tatami* (a woven rush mat) is the basis of all plan forms. The *tatami* measures approximately 1 m × 2m, in other words it is a rectilinear unit of two squares. Thus, half a mat is the basic planning module and room sizes are built up on that module. The *tatami* therefore reveal, in the floor pattern, the *Gestalt* of the room or the house, the characteristics of this pattern being subtly enhanced by the fact that the *tatami* take on a different 'shading' when they are placed parallel to a light source from that which they reveal when they are placed perpendicular to a light source.

The Japanese interior does not, however, transfer its 'unifying effect' to the exterior of the structure. In the outside world it is the discipline of the garden, of systematized nature, that provides the *Gestalt*. This in turn affords the contrast provided by the picture-window view from the interior. In the interior nature is merely suggested by a symbolic detail, such as an unplaned support or a bamboo/flower vase, just as from the outside the interior is hinted at by the details in the shade of the house eaves.

If we contrast this tradition in turn with the use of the square by, say, Walter Gropius or Louis Kahn, the plan expression is clean enough but the

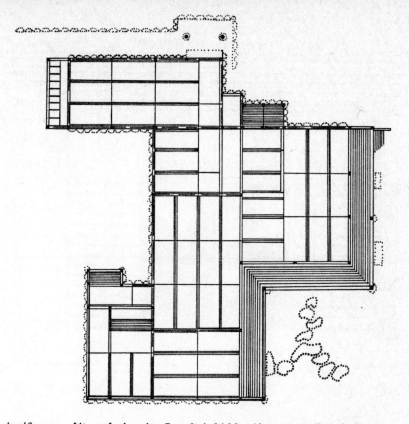

significance of its ordering, its *Gestalt*, is hidden if not actually missing.

If form is not to be mere formality it will have to satisfy certain conditions which are not themselves formalities. It is not enough to rely upon Sullivan's proposal that 'form follows function' since any number of forms might match a given function. A decision to use a square plan form, for example, is meaningless if the square plan does not generate a significant three-dimensional spatial organization.

Whether we are designing houses or aircraft there are a number of formal solutions which will meet the functional requirements more or less successfully: the tighter the performance specification the more limited will be the number of acceptable solutions. In the field of space exploration the performance specification has achieved a new clarity of definition. This clarity and extreme objectivity allows the design of spacecraft and equipment to fall within the simplistic formula that 'form follows function'. This is because we are not, at the moment, dealing with the whole environmental situation in space research: we are still at the early stage of considering only vehicles and equipment, at a primitive stage, in fact. This primitive stage has one advantage for our study: the question of aesthetics has not yet become pertinent in the area of space design.

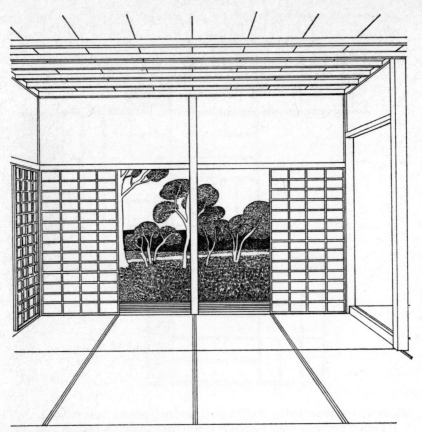

A *tokonoma* in the Katsura Palace, Kyoto.

Yet a style – that is to say a hierarchy of recognizable forms – is emerging from the functional requirements of space exploration. The interesting thing, I suggest, is that this style has not emerged from our way of life, it has no connexion with any of the patterns we have inherited or are generating in our daily lives: we are only aware of it indirectly through the media of television, film and stills, in other words it is beyond our experience.

Spacecraft represent an idealization of escape from the terrestrial limitations of our existence, which is one reason why they have figured so prominently in science fiction for the past hundred years. They operate in 'outer' space, that is, space which is outside our experience and, even if we are occasionally able to see actual examples in travelling exhibitions, they do not form part of our reality as do, for example, other sophisticated forms of travel such as jet aircraft, hovercraft, and even submarines. I

A master of the tea ceremony.

believe that this distinction between what falls within our sense of reality and what is excluded from it is important in our understanding of the design of our environment. Space travel exists today: i.e. we co-exist with it. But it is external to our cultural framework, and it will remain so for some considerable time except for those few pioneers who are working on the frontiers of knowledge and the exploration of the unknown.

This goes some way to explain why extreme fashions are not absorbed into our daily lives: it is simply that they are outside our experience and we therefore find them outlandish and unacceptable. We 'know about' many things that we do not understand, and we cannot absorb the incomprehensible into our lives, not in good faith at least. In other words the limits of our ability to interact with our culture are prescribed by the limits of our experience.

This is perhaps more clearly expressed by a German friend, who, when asked by pupils how long it will take them to learn German, replies simply: 'You will never get to know another language better than you know your own.' Utopia, the Ideal City – these are concepts beyond our cultural experience. Like the concept of space travel they are imposed from outside our evolutionary patterns.

For the moment I wish to concentrate on the examination of how we identify the limitations of the 'real' in environmental terms, because it is in this area of assessment that we establish the possibilities of cultural interaction. The consequences of this assessment are cohesiveness on the one hand and alienation on the other. Either we identify with some points within the limitations of the 'real' or we place ourselves beyond those limits. The choice beyond the limitations are invention, mysticism and anarchy: the first two attempt to expand the limits of the 'real', the third seeks its total destruction. For those who do not or cannot choose there is the extra-mural no-man's land of despair.

If we accept that our existence is limited by the confines of real experience we also accept that Man must be essentially a conservative animal, perhaps even that his approach to environmental design is based on maintaining the *status quo*, i.e. perfecting established patterns within carefully prescribed limits; is it not strange, therefore, that Man, the land-oriented animal, has consistently during the past five-hundred years devoted himself more to the problems of navigation and flight than to those of dwelling on land? It is for this reason that nautical and aeronautical science are specialist activities whereas architecture is not.

This state of affairs may have arisen because it has been assumed that the design of our environment falls within 'real' experience and therefore cannot be the subject of exploration. But this approach would have to be based on the passing from generation to generation of a consistently valid body of knowledge about the realities of environmental design. Barry Commoner quotes the case of the watchmakers, 'who over the years, each taught by a predecessor, have tried out a huge variety of detailed arrangements of watch works, have discarded those that are not compatible with the overall operation of the system and retained the better features . . . any random change made in the watch is likely to fall into the very large class of inconsistent, or harmful, arrangements which have been tried out in past watch-making experience and discarded. One might say, as a law of watches, that the watchmaker knows best.'[4] But one cannot say that of architects, who have not approached the problem of environmental control with the tenacity of the watchmaker, and who have managed to pass only limited information from generation to generation. The overruling reason for this is that the history of building is not the history of a single tradition but of continual rupture and fragmentation, with frequent loss of skills resulting from the imposition of alien patterns from outside sources. In other words, technological evolution and aesthetic movements are not necessarily complementary.

In a previous essay I used the term 'existential space' with reference to

Lao Tse's proposal that it was not the floor, walls and roof that constituted a building, but the space within those elements. That essay was written before the appearance of Norberg-Schultz's recent book *Existence, Space and Architecture*, and my use of the term 'existential' in relation to space was not therefore related to Professor Norberg-Schultz's. I shall return to the particularly existential aspects of space in the essay which appears on page 63, but in the interim it would, I believe, be helpful if I introduced at this point the five concepts (or aspects) of space as defined by Professor Norberg-Schultz, since these have a direct bearing on our present concern with real experience. These five are (1) the pragmatic space of physical action; (2) the perceptual space of immediate orientation; (3) the existential space which forms man's stable image of his environment; (4) the cognitive space of the physical world, and (5) the abstract space of pure logical relations.

Norberg-Schultz explains: 'Pragmatic space integrates man with his natural "organic" environment, perceptual space is essential to his identity as a person, existential space makes him belong to a social and cultural totality, cognitive space means that he is able to think about space, and logical space, finally, offers the tool to describe the others. The series shows a growing abstraction from pragmatic space at the lowest level to logical space at the top, that is, a growing content of "information". Cybernetically, thus, the series is controlled from the top, while its vital energy rises from the bottom.' My own use of the term 'existential' included, in these terms, the span of 'perceptual', 'existential' and 'cognitive', i.e. existential space to me is the space within which we exist and with which we interact. Norberg-Schultz describes this in the following way: 'From remote times man has not only acted in space, perceived space, existed in space and thought about space, but he has also created space to express the structure of his world as a real *imago mundi*. We may call this creation expressive or artistic space, and it finds its place in the hierarchy next to the top, together with cognitive space. Like cognitive space, expressive space needs a more abstract construct for its description, a space concept which systematises the possible properties of expressive spaces. We may call this "aesthetic space".' He then decides to call expressive space 'architectural space', with aesthetic space as the theoretical concept of architectural space. He goes on: 'In a certain sense, any man who chooses a place in his environment to settle and live, is a creator of expressive space. He makes his environment meaningful by assimilating it to his purposes at the same time as he accommodates to the conditions it offers.'

Only two paragraphs before, Norberg-Schultz had defined 'existential space' as 'Man's "image" of his environment, that is, a stable system of three-dimensional relations between meaningful objects'. With that one can only agree, and it corresponds to my own inclusion of his 'perceptual,' 'existential' and 'cognitive' in the one 'existential' package. Nevertheless it is obviously an advantage to break this comprehensive term down into

Sehzade Mosque, Istanbul (1543–48).

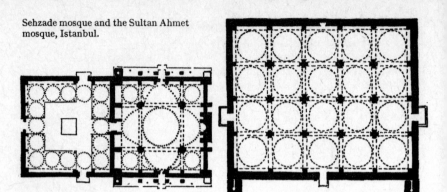

Sehzade mosque and the Sultan Ahmet mosque, Istanbul.

five conceptual stages, providing this hierarchy of concepts does not itself break down. In this respect the introduction of 'expressive' and 'artistic' are not helpful in terms of the original hierarchy as this allows the interchange of 'existential' and 'expressive'. Also these terms in turn merge into 'architectural', while the concept of 'existential' provides a useful way forward (in Lao Tse's terms) because it represents the interaction between 'being' and 'expression'. Realizing, perhaps, that he had gone astray from the 'path', Norberg-Schultz goes on to suggest: 'Obviously man's schemata are created through interaction with existing architectural spaces, and when these do not satisfy him, that is, when his image becomes confused or too unstable, he will have to change his architectural space. Architectural space, therefore, can be defined as a concretisation of man's existential space.'

Clearly what is important in the 'concretisation' of existential space is the selection of the means, the technology, the structural system: that is the basis of the formal expression and a measure of its significance. The abstract spatial concept of pure logical relations, i.e. circulation diagrams, functional analysis, even plans, must be translated into significant three-dimensional form by appropriate (expressive) structural means. Without mastery of structural language one will never master architectural expression. The student who is expert in the collection of relevant data and its analysis, in writing the brief, is still only capable of dealing with abstractions. Without the skill to progress from this abstract process to the perceptive, existential and cognitive stages he is unable to give reality to existential space simply because it is not real for him.

This was similarly expressed by Louis Kahn in a paper 'Form and Design' (1961): 'Reflect then on what characterises abstractly House, a house, home. House is the abstract characteristic of spaces, good to live in. House is the form; in the mind of wonder it should be there without shape or dimension. A house is a conditional interpretation of these spaces. This is design. In my opinion the greatness of the architect depends on his powers of realisation of that which is House, rather than his design of a house which is circumstantial act. Home is the house and its occupants. Home becomes different with each occupant.'

Elsewhere we have considered the *Gestalt* of the Japanese house as revealed in the *tatami* mats, with their format of the double square. But this squareness of the module (half-a-mat) was not directly transferred to the structural system and the expressiveness of the third dimension: rather it remains implicit in the floor, the foot-print, to use one of Louis Kahn's terms.

The square planning module in Ottoman architecture stems immediately from the logic of the structural system, the vaulted space, a series of vaulted spaces, a domed space or a series of domed spaces.

Sinan's first masterpiece, the Sehzade mosque in Istanbul (1543–48), is in many ways his most perfect in plan form – with its double square, one exterior, one interior – and in the careful modulation of the massing. The forecourt is the negative (open) space which is complemented by the positive (covered) interior space. In its build up of domes and half domes the Sehzade represents perfection of the Ottoman expression. Its plan is repeated in the Sultan Ahmet mosque in Istanbul, but Sinan's Suleymaniye mosque has a foreshortened courtyard, i.e. only five modules to the seven of the entrance façade.

The Ottoman architects had achieved the complete integration of a building's organizational system, its *Gestalt*, and its external form. The architectural order was no longer a hidden one, it was expressed: the system became the reality.

When the elephants were white!

We do not know exactly what was the nature of the rituals practised by the inhabitants of the Maltese islands during the Megalithic period or why it was that they chose to arrange their places of worship with the particular plan formations they selected, but whatever it was it produced a consistently coherent morphology.

The plans were 'closed systems', consisting of an entry passage or court which led directly into a central area, and around that central area were clustered a number of terminal spaces. The entrance space is normally square or rectilinear, the central space is of a circular or horseshoe form and the peripheral spaces are also a horseshoe in plan.

This general configuration of the plan is not unusual in primitive structures. It can be found, for example, in the organization of the various rooms of village houses at Damongo in Ghana as described by Charles Cockburn.[1] In fact the centralization of spatial organization, the development of 'closed systems' of dependencies which are related to and in turn enclose a central space, is common in the domestic, religious and defensive structures of most societies. To use a central space as the principal means of circulation is, of course, a basic planning strategy where problems of natural lighting and ventilation are of no particular relevance. But it is fairly evident that in the Maltese temples or shrines the central space was in fact central to the rituals.

A central, enclosed space, with its restricted access, assures maximum security, even secrecy. In this, in its fundamental form, it is also a concrete representation of sexual reality, namely the relationship between the vagina or access passage and the womb itself, which is to the primitive society the ultimate interior mystery of enclosure, of birth and death.[2] By penetrating into this interior volume we can share in the mystery of life and death, by re-enacting the sexual mystery we can connect ourselves with the inevitability of the life-death cycle. One of the architect's current design dilemmas, a central problem I suggest of Renaissance and post-Renaissance architecture, is that the development of knowledge and

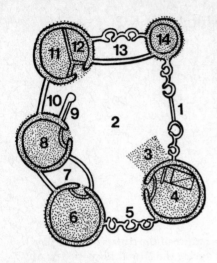

Fra-Fra house, Damongo.

Plan of John's house.
Key: 1. main entrance, 2. courtyard,
3. covered sitting area, 4. main sleeping room
5. nesting holes for hens, 6. store and
subsidiary sleeping room for children
7. section of the yard divided from the rest by
1 ft high wall which acts as a seat – peppers
were drying there, 8. flat-roofed stor-room,
9. seat moulded into tne wall, 10. coolihg
enclosure, 11. kitchen, 12. section walled off
for goats, 13. drained washing area, 14. forcal
house.

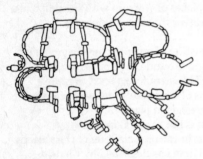

Left: Plan of temple at Taxien, Malta
Opposite: Temple at Hagar Qim, Malta.

communication has conspired to eliminate that which is mystical in our lives, i.e. other than 'real'. This means that we are left with a vocabulary of outmoded forms on the one hand and the resources of new structural technology on the other. But there is no system, either philosophical or cultural, to connect them.

The history of European architecture from its first manifestations to the end of the Middle Ages centres on a technological response to society's physical requirements married with artistic responses to the spiritual or mystical element in Man. The architect today suffers two disadvantages at the hands of society, viz. either the spiritual/mystical element is presumed to be no longer part of our present reality, or an attempt is made to conjure up that which is deep-rooted in human mythology by the superficial application of outmoded symbols which merely demonstrate the hollowness of *homo sapiens* today or the impoverished condition of his inner being.

For the purpose of my present argument let us look first at the significant form of the Maltese temples and the technology employed in

the realization of that form. There is sexual symbolism in the execution of
the enclosing elements as well as the plan, which is clearly demonstrated by
the phallic monoliths outside the oracle chamber and several internal
orifices. What is interesting and important in these examples is the
marriage of material available – colossal stone slabs – and the technology
by which it was formed into an homogeneous whole. The stone slabs were
put together to form 'closed system' buildings, not merely monuments.
It would have been relatively simple (after transporting the stone slabs,
each of which weighs several tons, over extremely difficult terrain!) to
erect a circle of monoliths. The builders of the temple at Hagar Qim were
aiming at a more sophisticated solution, however, and they achieved it by
tooling the edges of the rough slabs until they fitted together with a
precision that is extraordinary considering the limitations of the available
technology. This jointing of the stone slabs is all the more notable because
of the frequent use of extremely subtle curvatures at the junctions. This
use of curves was evidently of some significance to the society of the
Maltese islands during the Megalithic period. No similar structures have
been discovered in the Mediterranean area thus far, and the unique details
of form and curvature have been translated direct from the original form
of the surface structures to the 'formalism' of the later underground
complex of temples known as the Hypogeum, at Paola near Valletta.
Formalism demonstrates one of the fundamental weaknesses in the
perpetuation of a building system or its details when these have become
outmoded by technological change or the use of a different material. We
have made much of the beauty of the Parthenon, yet its detailing derives
from an archaic form of timber structure which was translated into the

'Fairy chimneys' in the Göreme Valley, Turkey.

artificial system of the Doric Order, i.e. the reproduction of an essentially wooden building form in stone, perpetuating what began as an expedient by making it into a permanent cultural form. This is perhaps an outstanding example of our assertion that 'art begins where technique ends'.

There are many examples of this perpetuation of a tradition outside its original context. An exact parallel to the Hagar Qim and Hypogeum case exists in the rock-cut monasteries of the Göreme Valley in Cappadocia, where once again the 'builders' or rock-carvers have exactly simulated the original built form, in their case the whole Byzantine tradition of columns, vaults and domes, with painted capitals and abacus blocks. But perhaps the most impressive example of all is to be found in the cave palaces of Ajanta, Hyderabad, dating from the fifth to seventh centuries.

Turning again to Hagar Qim we can observe the curious porthole penetration of one of the slabs, giving access from one chamber to another, a detail that is exactly reproduced in the central portion of the Hypogeum. Even more notable is the reproduction of the whole trabeated system of Hagar Qim and Mnajdra, which is stylized and carved into the solid rock of the 'Holy of Holies' at the Hypogeum. But there is still a link between the original form and style of the Hagar Qim and Mnajdra temples and their later stylistic adaptation in the underground vaults of the Hypogeum. That same link exists between the Byzantine tradition of vaulting over square bays and the virtual reproduction of the Byzantine style in the galleries and chimneys of the Göreme Valley. The link in both cases is the continuation of a ritual tradition for which the structures, both original and *ersatz*, were developed.

Today, in the Western world, we have neither the continuation of a ritual tradition nor the maintenance of traditional structural systems. This break with tradition, which in formal terms has its roots in the Renaissance of the quattrocento and in technological terms stems from the Industrial Revolution and the advent of skeletal structures, has given us the present paradox of a vocabulary of outmoded symbolic forms in conflict with a technology that generates dynamic rather than static structural solutions. As a student I found the fact that structural design was referred to as the study of statics one of the principal discouragements of the subject. In fact modern structural design is achieved by an understanding of dynamics, which is an important distinction and not merely a semantic one. This fact is clearly demonstrated by the work of Buckminster Fuller.

It is now possible to do almost anything structurally. In other words, a structure need not be the organic product of the plan form, neither is it necessary for the plan form to be a direct expression of the structural *Gestalt*. As I said earlier the *Gestalt* or *la psychologie de la forme* of the Japanese house is its planning module, based on a 1 metre square (i.e. half the double-square woven *tatami* mat); in other words it is a two-dimensional geometric generator, whereas in the Byzantine church and Ottoman mosque the *Gestalt* is the structural system of vaulting and domes, a three-dimensional space generator, with the result that a complete integration of architectural order and expression, both internally and externally, is achieved.

Today we live in an age of structural permissiveness. We may no longer respond to the comprehensive symbolism of sexual mystery, as the Megalithic society of the Maltese islands almost certainly did, but we may indulge instead in an orgy of unconnected and irrelevant form. Alan Colquhoun has commented upon this in his paper 'Symbolic and literal aspects of technology': [3]

'Every architect today is torn between two concepts of architecture. On the one hand architecture is seen to consist of unique works of art, the creation of individual sensibility, on the other it is seen as belonging to the public sphere, where private sensibility is under the control of "techniques" in the broad sense of the word.'

I suggest that this 'public sphere' concept describes the position of Megalithic society in the Maltese islands, and for that matter elsewhere, because all forms and expression were subject to the overall discipline of that society's symbolism and ritual. This position was, more or less, maintained until the end of the Middle Ages, although the purity of symbolism and ritual in post-Minoan civilizations (with which the Maltese Megalithic society was contemporary) became adulterated by migration. The Graeco-Buddhist confluence of the first and second centuries in India is another example of this adulteration of symbolism and style (Fig. 18).

Colquhoun continues: 'The fact that the technological and social revolution assumed by the Modern Movement did not take place brought to the surface the extent to which its work was the result of private will to form – and the extent to which all architecture must be so based. Once this is admitted the mystical link between art and technique was broken, and the architect was free to enlarge the theoretical context within which he designed. This link had been forged from a Utopian and eschatological view of society, art and technology which was no longer tenable. What inevitably followed was a more empirical attitude towards construction and researches into form which were fundamentally unconcerned with the problem of advanced techniques.'

In other words we have developed an attack of what I shall call the Pirandello syndrome. Pirandello, it will be remembered, wrote a play entitled *Six Characters in Search of an Author* and I suggest that the current architectural design dilemma stems as much as anything from the existence of at least six forms in search of any one function.

It would appear that the morphological configuration of the temples at Hagar Qim and Mnajdra stemmed directly from the concept of secrecy and security surrounding various sacred mysteries, with these mysteries of what T. S. Eliot described as the cycle of 'birth, copulation and death' themselves suggesting the sexual symbolism of the temple form. The central space at Hagar Qim and Mnajdra is central to the mystic symbolism of birth (the womb) and death (the grave). The connexion between the two is the mystery of copulation.

It will be noted that I refer to the 'mystery' of copulation. If we remove the sense of mystery from sex we strip Man of his 'inner spirit', i.e. his human spirit or 'soul', in other words all that is beyond the immediate experience of pleasure and pain. The truly erotic is an extension of the imagination beyond the actual experience, the 'fact' of sex is merely an animal experience. I suggest that the ecstatic experience of life which derives from its underlying mysteries tends to be cancelled out by the romance (or fiction) of what we have come to think of scientifically as 'facts'. Mystery requires a search beneath the surface, whilst a bombardment of 'facts' may tend to overexpose us to the mere superficialities of a situation.

In this way, largely as a consequence of the teaching of the history of architecture and art as a superficial ready-reference of visual imagery unaccompanied by a thorough grasp of its *Gestalt* and *Zeitgeist*, we have been overexposed to the possibilities of merely formal positions. This experience is entirely vicarious, rather like being at a strip-show where the propositions are made by the performer from a safe distance, where all the mystery has been removed but there is nothing available to take its place. It is perhaps not surprising, therefore, that many of our current architectural products amount in effect to formal titillation.

With the plan of the Maltese temples still in mind it is interesting to examine two English buildings of the 1960s, the Metropolitan Cathedral of

Detail of church entrance, Göreme Valley.

Christ the King, Liverpool, and the Elephant and Rhinoceros House at London Zoo (Figs.15, 17). In the cathedral we see that while the plan form closely resembles that of the temples the structure embodies a traditional mediaeval formula of a tower at the crossing, resulting in a tent-like form that has earned the building the colloquial name of Paddy's Wigwam. In the case of the zoo, however, the plan of the Elephant House resembles that of the Maltese temples and the structure has been restrained to a simple enclosing wall, with directional rooflight not unlike the pattern we have come to expect from post-Ronchamp religious buildings.

Elephant and Rhinoceros House, London Zoo
and Cathedral of Christ the King, Liverpool.

The sense of confinement which is achieved in the central 'visitor' area allows one to focus more sharply on the animal enclosures, located on a lower level so that one's eye goes down to them naturally. The building thus frames the extraordinary experience. What could be more extraordinary, more primordial, more redolent of mystery than the sight of those survivors of Man's early days, the elephant and the rhinoceros. And there they are in the chapel-like apses, complete with wrinkled skin, and other curiously symbolic details that could easily date from Genesis.

In the Metropolitan Cathedral, authentic details, with which the visitor can connect, are conspicuously absent. The plan is too open in the third dimension, the space always escaping just where it needs to be contained. This is particularly unfortunate since the closing of the central space – around its periphery at the threshold to the chapels – would have given greater emphasis to the soaring lantern.

It is in the lantern that the use of stained glass is most successful. The quality of light in the interior, reflecting the rapid changes in the Liverpool sky and weather, is the 'environmental detail' which relieves the barren surfaces on bright days and emphasizes the spiritual impoverishment on dull days. Unfortunately the stained glass in the drum and chapels does little to relieve the thoroughly mundane character, seeming as it does to seek its inspiration from those wishy-washy front door panels of semi-detached 'villas'. Religion is concerned with life and death, spanned by a bridge of optimism. In Gibberd's cathedral one's ecstasy is restrained to dreaming of suburbia. Perhaps in this sense it does represent to the Liverpudlian what *kitsch* does to the Portuguese peasant: both are merely a thin veneer of religion on a more earthy cultural substructure.

If I am right in this it means that the symbolic content of form *per se* no longer exists, and the significance of any particular form is now entirely subject to the arbitrary rules of the Pirandello game. This in turn would suggest that we have, most of us, been so overexposed to outmoded formal symbols that they no longer correspond to any particular functions.

The environmental memory

When the Duke of Wellington was asked whether he agreed that habit was
man's second nature he exclaimed: 'Second nature? It's ten times nature!'
It might be useful to think of design as breaking through one's nature in
order to come to grips with a problem; breaking existing habits in order to
acquire new ones. Koestler speaks of 'the bisociative pattern of creative
synthesis; the sudden interlocking of two previously unrelated skills, or
"matrices of thought"'. Perhaps one question that should concern us is:
how, in design education, can we actively encourage this interlocking
process? The academic system of the Beaux-Arts taught the student to
understand form by a kind of programmed learning, i.e. by drawing from
nature, the plaster cast and classical buildings. It was not an abstract,
theoretical study such as could be undertaken by reading about form: the
mind and therefore the memory was engaged in observing first, then using
one's observations as the starting point of a drawn record. In other words
there were no short cuts: what one had observed carefully one could draw
accurately, and what one had both observed and reproduced (employing
the skills of analysis and manual dexterity as the bridges between
observation and comprehension) was then stored in the archives of the
mind. These archives became the 'accumulated knowledge and experience
of what had been observed and recorded'. Because we see does not mean
that we understand: understanding requires a bit more effort. We see
through the lens of the camera, but having pressed the shutter release the
record is transferred to the film and not to our minds. This is the limitation
of the camera compared with the pen or pencil: the camera is merely a
mechanical device while the pencil in the hand is a direct extension of the
mind in action. In order to understand what one has recorded on the film
it is necessary to develop the film, study the negatives, make enlargements
of the whole or parts and so on. Then, and only then, will the original visual
organization re-emerge, making possible at the same time an understanding
of the image's structure and the manipulative potential of its component
parts.

Koestler has described a scale of creativity with 'more or less conscious reasoning' at one end and 'sudden insights which seem to emerge spontaneously from the depth of the unconscious' at the other. Now, these 'sudden insights', or what we sometimes refer to as 'intuitive flashes of inspiration', are what artists and architects, who might otherwise appear to be resting from their labours, often protest they are awaiting. In order to clear the air of some of the mystery and speculation that normally surrounds these moments of inspiration I shall attempt to define intuition as I understand it from personal experience and as it has been testified to by others.

Perhaps it would be appropriate if I left the world of artistic creativity for a moment and gave the evidence of three scientists, all quoted by Koestler in *The Act of Creation*. First, an anonymous mathematician: 'Most striking at first is this appearance of sudden illumination, a manifest sign of *long, unconscious prior work*. The role of this unconscious work in mathematical invention appears uncontestable.' Second, the Frenchman André Marie Ampère (after whom the unit of electric current is named): 'I gave a shout of joy . . . It was seven years ago I proposed to myself a problem which I have not been able to solve directly, but for which I found *by chance* a solution, and knew that it was correct, without being able to prove it.' (In fact the mathematical knowledge necessary to prove Ampère's theory was not available at the time he formulated it. Similarly, the inspired 'hunch' to conclude Schubert's 'Unfinished' Symphony with music from *Rosamunde* at a Crystal Palace concert in 1881 was not supported by material evidence until half a century later.) Third, the mathematician Karl Friedrich Gauss, describing in a letter to a friend how he finally proved a theorem whose solution had eluded him for four years: 'At last, two days ago, I succeeded, not by dint of *painful effort* but so to speak by the Grace of God. As a sudden flash of light, the enigma was solved . . . For my part I am unable to name the nature of the *thread* which connected what I had previously known with that which made my success possible.'

The italics for (1) long, unconscious prior work, (2) by chance, (3) painful effort, and (4) thread, are my own. The awareness of 'long, unconscious prior work' was very much in the mind of Ampère, who confesses: 'I do not know how I found it together with a large number of curious and new considerations concerning the theory of probability.' Gauss tends to dismiss the years of unconscious painful effort and, failing to find a thread, credits the supernatural, i.e. the Grace of God. Clearly even 'divine inspiration' depends upon prior work. We have, of course, Edison's definition of genius as 'one per cent inspiration and ninety-nine per cent perspiration' and I suggest that it doesn't much matter whether the work or effort was conscious or unconscious; in either case it had been fed into the brain's data bank as a bit of information or a piece of experience from which information could be sifted.

When I was teaching at the Bartlett School of Architecture we were always weighing the relative merits of rationalization versus intuition and this led me to define 'intuition' for the purposes of my own investigations as 'instant recall of accumulated knowledge and experience, and its application out of the original contexts'. Thus, to like something or someone intuitively would mean responding to qualities or properties that have previously given pleasure in other objects or persons. This calls into question the concept of empathy as spontaneous response, because we can clearly be conditioned out of liking something which originally stimulated our pleasure or approval: we have only to look at the Pavlovian technique used to condition children in Huxley's *Brave New World*. So it would appear that both 'empathy' and 'intuition' depend upon the application of previous knowledge and experience. We may have a propensity towards brunettes, but know by experience that we fare better with blondes. Koestler in *The Act of Creation* relates creativity to the interlocking of two different planes of reference, one consisting of 'abilities, habits, and skills' and the other being 'patterns of ordered behaviour governed by fixed rules'. He gives an example of this 'interlocking' from the insect world: 'The common spider will suspend its web on three, four, and up to 12 handy points of attachment, depending on the lie of the land, but the radial threads will always intersect the laterals at equal angles, according to a fixed code of rules built into the spider's nervous system; and the centre of the web will always be at its centre of gravity. The web-building skill is flexible: it can be adapted to environmental conditions; but the rules of the code must be observed and set a limit on flexibility. The spider's choice of suitable points of attachment for the web are a matter of strategy, depending on the environment, but the form of the completed web will always be polygonal, determined by the code. The exercise of a skill is always under dual control (A) of a fixed code of rules (which may be innate or acquired by learning) and (B) of a flexible strategy, guided by environmental pointers – the "lie of the land".'

This marriage of skill and strategy employed by the spider in web-building seems to parallel the creative synthesis employed by the architect in designing buildings. In the architect's case the building skill, i.e. his knowledge of structural systems, building technology and their formal consequences, provides a code of rules: the disposition of the building on the ground and the employment of a particular built form are matters dependent upon environmental conditions and the client's brief which are amalgamated together into a flexible strategy.

It is the nature of this 'flexible strategy' that Christopher Alexander and his colleagues are trying to come to grips with in their concept of 'pattern language', pointing out that a given set of words in the English language plus a given set of grammatical rules can, in the hands of a poet, produce an infinite variety of sentences and poems: this is exactly paralleled by the building design process. Alexander himself says: 'Where an ordinary language is a system which generates one-dimensional strings (of words) called sentences, a "pattern language" is a natural generalisation of the idea to three dimensions.' Of course, sentences also have an emotive dimension which, through what Koestler calls 'bisociative synthesis', projects meanings beyond those necessarily intended by word and sentences as simple statements. This could be a limitation of 'pattern language' since, as I understand Alexander's conception, its vocabulary is not complete in formal terms and can therefore generate three-dimensional results only in terms of plan configuration. One interesting question is: 'Would it be possible for a code of rules about "formal language" to be activated by the flexible strategy of "pattern language"?' This question could stimulate a valuable research programme within the educational context.

It might be useful to consider creative synthesis as described by the writer Georges Simenon in an interview with *The Observer*, 23 May 1971.[1] He says: 'When I feel a novel coming on I put myself in a "state of grace". I empty myself of all the things I have in my mind. I take walks, I play golf. I think about the atmosphere I wish to have in this novel. When I have that I think about the characters. I ask myself what situations of stress I can put this man or woman into that will oblige them to go to their limits. It is often a very simple thing, an accident, a love affair – anything that will change their lives. And then I draft a few notes on the back of an envelope: the names of the characters, their ages, where they live, their telephone numbers. I speak to no one. Next morning I start. I have no plot when I begin. I know nothing about what will occur, just the situation and the characters. But that's the point, you understand. I become one of my characters, always the one who is driven to the limit. I feel what he feels and after eight days I am exhausted.'

What Simenon is describing is the code or 'pattern language' of his novels: the plot is his 'flexible strategy'. In my view the most significant factors in Simenon's description of his working method are his emphasis on (1) no preconception of plot, and (2) his complete involvement with the characters. The architect's responsibility in the design process is similar in that he must avoid preconceptions based on the 'formal language' alone, waiting until the correct 'formal' response is set off by the stimulus of the 'pattern language'. In other words the architect has to identify with the building-user (the character) and society at large (the reader) rather than with his own self-indulgent tendencies. Or, in Simenon's words, 'become one of the characters, always the one who is driven to the limit'.

Wittgenstein attacked the self-indulgent tendency in the artist in his letter to Norman Malcolm, discussing Tolstoy whom he greatly admired: 'I once tried to read *Resurrection* but couldn't. You see, when Tolstoy just tells a story he impresses me infinitely more than when he addresses the reader. When he turns his back on the reader then he seems to me most impressive. It seems to me his philosophy is most true when it's latent in the story.' This observation is certainly a cornerstone of literary criticism and also provides a valuable warning for architects.

To demonstrate another way in which the strategy and the code interlock Koestler cites the game of chess. 'A player looking at an empty board with a single bishop on it does not see the board as a uniform mosaic of black and white squares, but as a kind of magnetic field with lines of force indicating the bishop's possible moves. The code which governs the strategy can be put into simple mathematical equations which contain the essence of the pattern in a compressed "coded" form; or it can be expressed by a word, e.g. "diagonals". The code is the fixed invariable factor in the game, the strategy its variable aspect. *The two words* [Koestler uses 'matrix' for strategy throughout but I wished to avoid the introduction of a further term] *do not refer to different entities, they refer to different aspects of the same activity.* When you sit in front of the chess board your code is the rule determining which moves are permitted, your strategy is the total of possible choices before you.' Lastly, the choice of the actual move among the variety of permissible moves is a matter guided by the 'lie of the land' – the environment of other chessmen on the board. We have seen that comic effects are produced by the sudden clash of incompatible interlocking: to the experienced chess player a rook moving bishopwise is decidedly amusing, just as Mannerist architecture is 'funny' in terms of classical architecture.

I have italicized 'the two words do not refer to different entities; they refer to different aspects of the same activity' because it seems to me that this is where many design theories have gone wrong, i.e. they have either been concerned with 'formal language' as the code of rules, or with 'pattern language' as the strategy and with each to the exclusion of the other. It has been a chicken and egg situation, or in pre-Hegelian terms it has been assumed that theory preceded rather than coincided with the cause-effect chain. Koestler's analysis of chess seems perfectly to describe an ideal form of design activity, in which the designer would be acting as a kind of self-programming computer, responding via the code and strategy to the 'pattern language' stimuli of the problem.

There are some snags, however, before we can achieve this ideal state of working. Clearly it is possible to determine the 'pattern language' for any building type (with variation for size and complexity) but our ability to *learn* the 'formal language' must depend upon 'prior work' and 'painful effort'. The quality of modern architecture (like the architecture of all previous periods) is directly proportional to the amount of study that precedes the creative synthesis in the design process. Thus, the designer with inadequate preparation for the task in hand could not claim to be waiting for 'intuitive' inspiration: from an existentialist point of view this would obviously be a case of acting in 'bad faith'. Chess can only be played successfully by (1) knowledge of the code of rules, (2) study of the great games in history, and (3) practice. Like architecture it cannot be treated as a guessing game by serious players.

Language and meaning

Among the other fashions so readily embraced by modern architects we must include that of obscuring the philosophic issues of architectural intention and form with mumbo-jumbo. This is a dangerous process since it can serve only to alienate both clients and society at large. At the outset of this discussion, therefore, we might do well to remind ourselves of what Wittgenstein wrote of propositions in the *Tractatus Logicus Philosophicus* (4,021): 'a proposition is a picture of reality: for if I understand a proposition, I know a situation that it represents. And I understand the proposition without having had its sense explained to me.'

Wittgenstein's statement entails that a person can understand a proposition even if he has never seen or heard it before, even if the sense of it has never been explained to him; so that everyone who understands the language in which the proposition is written will understand it, providing the meanings of the constituent words are known to him.

On this basis it could be argued that all 'propositions' in classical architecture are repetitions of one statement, i.e. 'I am symmetrical, regulated and proportionally correct, therefore I am beautiful.' In other words the constituent parts of any order are always the same, and the organization of the constituent parts is not allowed much variety by the 'rules' of that order. That is the meaning of 'order'; that the constituent parts should be ordered.

The aim of the High Renaissance architects in Italy was to re-establish this order in architectural language: the aim of the Mannerist architects, on the other hand, was to use the constituent parts of the classical language with obvious grammatical and syntactical errors. We see the constituent parts of classical vocabulary in Mannerist buildings but they have been used outside the context of the rules. In classical terms, therefore, a Mannerist proposition could be seen as an absurd or comic statement, but not as a statement of classical 'truth'. But the Mannerist building is not a false statement *in toto*: it is a statement of fact, but not a statement of classical fact. In other words, Mannerists, seeking innovation within the

Gargoyle at Nuremberg, Germany.

language at their disposal, contrived to make statements which would not be permitted within the strict rules of the classical language of architecture. But Mannerist statements are not a *patois*, a dialect of classical language, they are absurd and comic statements. In linguistic terms we can parallel the sort of thing the Mannerists did in building. Let us take for example the Church's proposition that: 'The essential purpose of marriage is the procreation of the family.' The music-hall joke based on this proposition is: 'Marriage is essential: no family should be without it.' The first is a statement of 'truth', the second is an inversion of that 'truth'.

Perhaps the main contribution that Mannerism made to the development of architecture was in making the architectural joke a central rather than an incidental event. The gargoyle at Nuremberg is an incidental 'joke' in that its existence is an extension of the Gothic language. Giulio Romano's Palazzo del Tè is an all-inclusive 'joke' in classical terms. But the essence of a joke is that it must be comprehensible. The Mannerist joke is comprehensible because it makes howlers in relation to classical language, just the kind of howlers we used to enjoy at school in the weekly issues of *Acta Diurna*.

After Mannerism appeared in Italy architectural comic effects really got under way, becoming in time and especially with the advent of the academies increasingly esoteric and incomprehensible to all but a few *cognoscenti*. So we have reached a Joycean situation in architectural 'language' (the Joyce of *Finnegan's Wake* rather than *Ulysses*, the latter being still accessible via classical and Catholic channels). But we have no Stuart Gilbert to guide us through the murky waters of modern architectural language.

Is it possible for us to agree on what is good design and what is bad design, what gives us pleasure and what does not, what is beautiful and what is ugly? The whole basis of the classical language of architecture is that we must know the grammar and syntax before we are able to appreciate whether a building conforms to the rules and is therefore a 'good' building in the classical sense. In other words we cannot fully respond to it unless we understand the language of its form. The same would be true of the Japanese *haiku* poem. Our response is not allowed to be arbitrary because the artifact is not itself arbitrary. But Kant rejected this preconditioning of pleasurable responses outright, he differentiated the aesthetic experience – to him a mode of direct awareness – from all forms of conceptual thinking. In rational terms he made it clearer than it had ever been before that a thing cannot be proved to be beautiful on the ground that it belongs to a certain class of things (e.g. to Mediterranean peoples the blonde woman is a symbol of beauty, therefore, all blonde women must be beautiful to Italians) or has certain definable characteristics. Even perfection within a group or kind was not proof of beauty to Kant. He maintained that the notion of perfection involves a prior concept of the sort of thing it should be, the sort of properties such a thing should have. In judging a thing to be perfect we make an intellectual assessment that it conforms to a high degree with this prior concept and we are not, therefore, making a judgement about our feelings towards it in our awareness of it, consequently our judgement is not an aesthetic one. In Kant's terms a jeweller's appreciation of a diamond and an architect's appreciation of classical architecture have nothing to do with aesthetics.

Kant further made a distinction between 'internal purposiveness' (i.e. assessment of beauty independent of canons of judgement) and 'dependent' beauty (assessed with reference to predetermined standards of function or performance), a distinction already made by Hogarth. He overlooked the possibility that the object which conforms to intellectually predetermined laws may still give spontaneous pleasure, in other words he failed to recognize that cumulative exposure to established standards, intellectual or other, can affect and modify one's ability to respond spontaneously. From this point of view conventional education can be seen as a deliberate

attempt to prejudice responses and attitudes, which is one reason why
it is currently so much under attack from the younger generation and
even some members of the older generation.

Kant did, however, touch on the possibility of a link between
intellectually preconditioned and spontaneous responses in his concept
of 'the free and unimpeded interplay of imagination and understanding'.
In this he distinguished two categories of ideas, the rational and aesthetic.
Rational or intellectual ideas refer to transcendental concepts to which
experience can never be fully adequate (e.g. heaven, hell, eternity,
creation, etc.), straining after something lying out beyond the confines
of experience. By the use of the imagination the poet and artist try to
'body them forth', to find concrete expression more adequate and complete
than experienced nature can achieve. This parallels Schelling's view that:
'In art the infinite enters into the finite, the transcendental and the
inexpressible lie open to the grasp of the senses. Both philosophers and
artists penetrate the essence of the universe and break through the
barriers between the actual and the ideal; but the artist alone presents
the Absolute concretely, visibly to perception.'

The question, then, is 'What is perceived, and how, and with what
emotional or other response?' Wilhelm Worringer in his essay 'Abstraktion

Palazzo del Tè, Mantua, by Giulio Romano.

und Einfühlung' of 1908 writes: 'Aesthetic enjoyment is objectified self-enjoyment. To enjoy aesthetically means to enjoy myself in a sensuous object diverse from myself, to emphasise myself into it.' And he goes on to quote from Lipps's *Aesthetik*: 'Only in so far as this empathy exists are forms beautiful. Their beauty is this, the ideal freedom with which I live myself out in them. Conversely, form is ugly when I am unable to do this, when I feel myself inwardly unfree, inhibited, subject to a constraint in the form, or in its contemplation.'

So Worringer's view of aesthetic appreciation, like Kant's, is that it is entirely subjective. It is therefore interesting to note how he records the contrasting effect upon himself of Doric and Ionic temple architecture. 'The earnest and majestic monumentality of the Doric temple, which, with its unapproachable, supra-human abstraction, weighed down the terrestrial and gave it to feel the nothingness of its humanity, is no longer to be found in the Ionic temple. Despite all its majesty and despite its gigantic masses, it stands in closer relationship to man. It rises up serene and pleasant, replete with self-confident life and striving which, tempered by a marvellous harmony, appeals with gentle force to our sense of life. The laws of its construction are, of course, still the laws of matter, but its inner life, its expression, its harmony fall within the regularity of the organic. The compactness and rigidity of the Doric temple has been broken through; the proportions come closer to human or universally organic proportions, the columns have grown taller and more slender, they seem to arise aloft by their own force and at their topmost extremities willingly to allow themselves to be pacified by the pediment construction. Whereas in the Doric temple the lofty, expressionless law of matter in its exclusivity frightens away all human empathy, in the Ionic temple all the sensations of life flow uninhibitedly in, and the joyfulness of the stones irradiated with life becomes our own joy.'

The Parthenon, Athens.

On my first visit to Liverpool's Metropolitan Cathedral (Fig.17), I wrote in my notebook: 'Having no clear beginning, no real reference to the ground, its abutments rise at a rakish angle with an almost drunken lurch, then by contortions which have neither sensuous form nor structural integrity it proceeds upwards at an uncomfortable tilt, not so much with a celestial goal in mind but more "a sky's the limit" stance. A tawdry thing, trying to stretch too little too far, it is more like a stage-set designed to be seen mostly in the dark then left out in error in broad daylight. Since it is a tent for praying in, a more nomadic structure would have shown the dimension of man's brief hour of strutting than this gross exaggeration of his petty ambition.' Not a criticism of the building, perhaps, but my spontaneous non-empathetic reaction.[1]

I asked myself, in Schelling's terms, 'Does this building penetrate the essence of the universe and break through the barriers between the actual and the ideal?' which I felt were the qualities a cathedral should express. Unfortunately, this building does not say 'cathedral' to me. It says 'sky-line', yes, and 'stage-prop': to Liverpudlians it says 'Mersey Funnel' and 'Paddy's Wigwam'. But is that not what the Church wanted: a cheap symbol of grandeur? And was not the worthy Gibberd led like Engels before him (in his cathedral for Helsinki) to stretch a classical plan into a Gothic profile? It's the damned clients, you see. They always expect an architect to make a silk-purse out of a sow's ear. Or is it the other way about?

So in understanding the language of architecture we can respond to intellectual preconditioning or to spontaneous empathy, or even a mixture of both. The semiologists are trying to throw some light on the problem and Roland Barthès suggests: 'The aim of semiological research is to reconstitute the functioning of the systems of significations other than language in accordance with the process typical of any structuralist activity, which is to build a simulacrum of the objects under observation.'[2] As Geoffrey Broadbent says, it is perfectly possible to get at Barthès' meaning, but why make the effort? For my part I remain unconvinced that the effort would 'help show the fly the way out of the fly-bottle'.

Gillo Dorfles in his *Simbolo, Communicazione, Consumo* (1959) is more helpful. 'The problems of architecture, if considered in the same way as the other arts, as a "language", are the basis for a whole new current of thought, which allows it to be treated in terms of information and communication theory; and the meaning can be treated as a process which connects objects, events and beings with "signs", which evoke these very objects, events and beings. The cognitive process lies in our ability to assign meaning to the things around us, and this is possible because the "signs" are links between our own consciousness and the phenomenological world.'

I suggest that when the 'form' emanates from 'ritual' we have a better chance of recognizing the 'signs' and making the links. In other words the symbol or image becomes the environment.

Dorfles continues: 'So signs are the first and immediate tools of every communication. I am sure of one thing: architecture, like every other art, must be considered as an organic whole and, to a certain extent, institutionalised ensemble of signs, which can be partially identified with linguistic structures.' That is the best argument I have so far found to give 'linguistic' support to my contentions concerning ritual and form. Paolo Portoghese expresses a parallel view in his book *Borromini* (1969). 'Architecture is a language insofar as it is "a system of signs" used according to conventional rules which it obeys, and which, in the act of producing the real object, recreate and modify. Or we might say that in the process of architectural communication, and artistic communication in general, that which really counts, that from which it is possible to deduce a value judgement, is solely the communication of the structure. This conclusion indicates that we must consider architecture as an autonomous system of communication, with clearly identifiable methods and laws. Alongside an idea that tends to identify itself with verbal language there thus exists an architectonic idea, a system of mental processes capable of being translated into working operations and concrete objects, but not capable of becoming a significant part of the social and cognitive reality.'

The debate continues and will continue so long as we have 'restricted' and 'elaborated' speech patterns in our spoken and written languages.[2]

(Ad)Venturi(sm): pragmatism and/or empiricism?

Robert Venturi is a paradoxical figure in architectural practice and academicism. His book *Complexity and Contradiction in Architecture* has been regarded by some as his *apologia pro vita sua*, merely obscuring with more complexity and contradiction his own already contradictory and complex architectural expression. This is not altogether a fair criticism, if a criticism at all. Serlio, Vignola, Palladio, Scamozzi and Le Corbusier all published their own designs with the calculated intention of broadcasting their ideas. The difficulty arises in that, whereas it could be argued that Venturi's concepts and realizations need exposition, students of design might justifiably maintain that clarification is the first objective of exposition, while *Complexity and Contradiction* merely footnotes the existence and validity of such complexities and contradictions.

On the surface, therefore, Venturi is Mannerist in his executed works and a mystic in the defence of his *raison d'être*. In fact, reason would seem to be far from his world: his view of architectural language, its grammar and syntax, is that of a polyglot who is not wedded to any particular linguistic tradition and who might very well carry on his correspondence in a number of languages, picking the best words from each source, accepting, for example, that terms like *Gestalt* and *Zeitgeist* do not exist in English and that *psychologie de la forme* and *esprit* might be clumsy or inaccurate. Certainly his expository style reflects that this is his attitude towards images and concepts within visual and spatial language. But I should like to offer some explanation of Venturi's book in the wider cultural and creative context of design education, that is leaving aside whether or not it helps us better to understand either Venturi or his buildings.

My view, simply stated, is that Venturi has written an anti-academic treatise. In other words although his book is a treatise in the traditional academic sense it is in fact an indictment of the academic system with its emphasis on rational method and the encapsulating of particular traditions or 'grammars' in isolation from all others.

For example, in his preface to *Complexity and Contradiction* he quotes

David Jones as saying[1] that '... because the arts belong to the practical and not the speculative intelligence, there is no surrogate for being on the job'. He hopes that: 'The architect's ever diminishing power and his growing ineffectualness in shaping the whole environment can perhaps be reversed, ironically, by narrowing his concerns and concentrating on his own job.' He reminds us that Summerson in *Heavenly Mansions* had already drawn attention to the architect's obsession with 'the importance, not of architecture, but of the relation of architecture to other things',[2] substituting the 'mischievous analogy' for an eclectic imitation of the nineteenth century and concentrating on staking a claim for architecture rather than producing it. Venturi then proceeds to devote eighty pages to his exposition and defence of complexity and contradition in architecture, particularly his own, while only thirty pages are left for the illustration and discussion of his own work. I suggest that it is this emphasis on what appears at first glance to be a defence of his own personal approach to design that prompts critics to suggest that the wider applications of his observations are not valid.

Again in the preface he remarks: 'I accept what seem to me architecture's inherent limitations, and attempt to concentrate on the difficult particulars within it rather than the easier abstractions about it.' Here we see the basic paradox and the essential ambiguity of Venturi's approach. If we are to take him at face value *Complexity and Contradiction* is a personal sketchbook, with those eighty pages of the *apologia* included merely as a background to his own projects. This would explain the absurdly small 'thumb-nail sketch' illustrations in the margins of the book, and it is a view substantiated by his quoting from Ackerman that Michelangelo rarely adopted a motif in his architecture 'without giving it a new form or a new meaning. Yet he invariably retained essential features from ancient models in order to force the observer to recollect the source while enjoying the innovations.'[3] T. S. Eliot is also brought in as a witness, with his observation that poets employ 'that perpetual slight alteration of language, words perpetually juxtaposed in new and sudden combinations',[4] with Wordsworth's additional evidence from the preface to his *Lyrical Ballads* of choosing 'incidents and situations from common life (so that) ordinary things should be presented to the mind in an *unusual* aspect'.

This desire to disturb the 'audience', i.e. unsettle its mental or emotional complacency, was a characteristic device of the Italian Mannerists as demonstrated in Tintoretto's *Massacre of the Innocents* and *The Finding of the Body of St Mark*. This disturbing component of art was formally expressed by Diderot in 1766 when he wrote that: 'The arts of imitation must have something wild, primitive, striking and monstrous ... in the first place move me, surprise me, rend my heart, make me tremble, weep, shudder, outrage me.'[5] It is this emphasis on the 'unexpected' that characterizes Venturi's search for form, and it is his central 'message' as far as I am concerned. Clearly, the student's experience is enriched if he is able to observe and record 'the surprise', 'the unexpected', 'the unusual' feature, but to do this his basic sensitivity must already be alert to what is 'regular', 'uniform', and 'acceptable' within the language of architecture and urban design. This alertness to, or awareness of, normality is essential in the first instance if a merely fashionable cult of the abnormal is not to supplant a proper investigation of form and content in architecture. Architecture, on the complexity level, is analogous with poetry in that as Phil Virden says: 'Besides the usual language relationships, poetry conveys the message by word order, loaded metaphors, coloured words, phonetic and rhythmic relationships and stanza form. With poetry, far more than with prose, every aspect and relationship can carry meaning. Poetry conveys meaning through the form so here the form/content distinction stands revealed for what it is – an analytic distinction.'[6]

Here lies the heart of the anti-academism in Venturi's thesis, for his argument, as are his concern and personal search, is based on the non-acceptance of a standard set of rules concerned with how architecture 'is' or 'should be' THIS or THAT. The only problem is that, in the case of Venturi's own work, the exception does often prove to be the rule.

He rightly argues that: 'The Doric temple's simplicity to the eye is achieved through the famous subtleties and precision of its distorted geometry and the contradictions and tensions inherent in its order. The Doric temple could achieve apparent simplicity through real complexity. When complexity disappeared, as in the late temples, blandness replaced simplicity.' And again: 'Blatant simplification means bland architecture. Less is a bore.' When he turns his attention to our own period he is able to underline our own dilemma. 'An architecture of complexity and contradiction, however, does not mean picturesqueness or subjective expressionism. A false complexity has recently countered the false simplicity of an earlier modern architecture. It promotes an architecture of symmetrical picturesqueness – which Minoru Yamasaki calls "serene" – but it represents a new formalism as unconnected with experience as the former cult of simplicity. Its intricate forms do not reflect genuinely complex programs, and its intricate ornament, though dependent on industrial techniques for execution, is dryly reminiscent of forms originally created by handicraft techniques. Gothic tracery and Rococo *rocaille* were not only expressively valid in relation to the whole, but came from a valid showing-off of hand skills and expressed a vitality derived from the immediacy and individuality of the method. This kind of complexity through exuberance, perhaps impossible today, is the antithesis of "serene" architecture, despite the superficial resemblance between them. But if exuberance is not characteristic of our art, it is tensions, rather than "serenity", that would appear to be so.'

Tension, a hidden tension, is indeed inherent in the apparent order of the Doric temple, a tension which is absent from the more superficially complex Ionic and Corinthian styles. Venturi quotes S. E. Hyman on Empson's view of ambiguity as 'collecting precisely at the points of greatest poetic effectiveness, and finds it breeding a quality he calls "tension" which we might phrase as the poetic impact itself'. Venturi believes that this definition might apply equally well to architecture: it surely applies to all art forms. But the ability to identify the tensions or ambiguities is quite a different matter from the ability to apply the lessons of those examples. Perhaps it is in a mood of self-criticism, therefore, that Venturi quotes Empson as admitting that: '(ambiguity) may be used to convict a poet of holding muddled opinions rather than to praise the complexity of the order of his mind'.[8]

It is appropriate that Venturi goes on to a consideration of Donne, whose complexity consisted in part of the 'tension' between his love poetry and his religious spirit. He quotes Cleanth Brooks' reference to Donne as 'having it both ways', whereas 'most of us in this latter day cannot. We are disciplined in the tradition either–or, and lack the mental agility – to say nothing of the maturity of attitude – which would allow us to indulge in the finer distinctions and the more subtle reservations permitted by the tradition of both–and.'[9] Venturi asserts that the tradition of 'either–or' has characterized orthodox modern architecture – 'a sun screen is probably nothing else; a support is seldom an enclosure; a wall is not violated by window penetrations but is totally interrupted by glass; program functions are exaggeratedly articulated into wings or segregated separate pavilions. Even "flowing space" has implied being outside when inside, and inside when outside, rather than both at the same time. Such manifestations of articulation and clarity are foreign to an architecture of complexity and contradiction, which tends to include "both–and" rather than exclude "either–or".' It is in this passage in particular, I think, that Venturi takes his strongest stand against academic rationalism and moves towards a "logical-negativism'. He begins with the clear statement of the 'either–or' and the 'both–and' from Cleanth Brooks, then removes the distinction, the valve if you like, by the introduction of the concept 'flowing space'. What is left is an entirely 'liquid' situation beneath the surface tension of the argument. In other words the logic can flow into the non-logic and vice versa, so that Venturi can, like Donne, have it both ways: or again, in the terms of the Zen question, he can propose that there will be a sound resulting from one-hand clapping just as there is a sound from two-hand clapping. It is in this sense that I class him as a mystic. Of course, Venturi is not short of 'both–and' examples which he can quote. Borromini's work abounds in instances of this type of formal complexity, of which San Carlo alle Quattre Fontane and Sant'Ivo in Sapienza are two of the best known examples of contradiction between façade and internal arrangement or function. Similarly, in Hawksmoor's St George's, Bloomsbury (Fig.19), the pedimented porch and overall plan shape imply a dominant north-south axis, whereas the entrance through the base of the tower opposite the east-end apse gives an equally dominant counter axis, providing a tension between the Latin Cross (front, back, and sides) and the duo-directional axes of the Greek cross in plan. Once one picks up the basic concept of 'both–and' it is not difficult to find the same tension in Palladio's 'Il Redentore' (temple and basilica in one) and Gaudí's 'Sagrada Familia' (superficially Gothic but resulting from a completely novel and non-mediaeval structural solution), even in the main chimneys on Lutyens's house Grey Walls (singled out for their double role as sculptural entrance marker buoys). All this soon begins to suggest the framework for a sort of architectural 'games people play', but Venturi has more or less tired of it by the time he gets to the end of chapter 7, where he concludes: 'It seems our fate now to be faced with either the endless inconsistencies of roadtown [i.e. continuous strip development along a highway], which is chaos, or the infinite consistency of Levittown, which is boredom. In a roadtown we have a false complexity; in Levittown a false simplicity. One thing is clear – from such false consistency real cities will never grow. Cities, like architecture, are complex and contradictory.'

The theme is now repeated on a deeper note and this gives Venturi more scope for development in the later chapters. Already at the beginning of chapter 6 he has sounded the clarions of the open society/system. 'A valid order accommodates as well as imposes. It thereby admits "control and spontaneity", "correctness *and* ease" – improvisations within the whole. It tolerates qualifications and compromise. There are no fixed laws in architecture, but not everything will work within a building or a city.' Note the 'as-well-as' in relation to accommodating and imposition, and the tolerance of 'qualification' and 'compromise'. He asks: 'Should we not look for the meaning in the complexities and contradictions of our times and acknowledge the limitations of systems?' He puts forward two justifications for breaking 'order': (1) the recognition of variety and confusion inside and outside, in programme and environment, at all levels of experience; and (2) the ultimate limitation of all orders composed by man. He concludes that: 'When circumstances defy order, order should bend or break; anomalies and uncertainty give validity to architecture.'

I agree with the concept of uncertainty as an essential aspect of the search for form (or 'order') and I shall return to this problem on page 113. This uncertainty (or 'indeterminacy') is as much a part of the solution as it is of the 'program', i.e. the function/performance specification of the problem. But even within such an open-ended system of 'delimitation' some resolution must be made if we are to go forward. Venturi agrees that: 'The architect must decide, and these subtle evaluations (i.e. 'control', 'spontaneity', 'correctness', 'ease', 'qualification' and 'compromise') are among his principal functions. He must determine what must be made to work and what is possible to compromise with, what will give in and where and how. He does not ignore or exclude inconsistencies of program and structure within the order.'

In other words the 'contradictions' are adapted within the 'order' and become part of it, a visible or invisible component of the overall 'tension' of the whole. But in chapter 8 Venturi discusses 'contradictions juxtaposed' in which contradictions are visibly apparent: 'its contradictory

Bank in Philadelphia by Frank Furness
(demolished).

relationships become manifest in discordant rhythms, directions, adjacencies, and especially in what I shall call superadjacencies – the superimpositions of various elements' (Fig.20). This interest is, in fact, Venturi's Achilles' heel since it is the one which is most evident in his own built forms, where the role of mystic is submerged in the play of exterior surface tensions, which having little of the depth of their historical paradigms, appear as a shallow manifestation of such a deep investigation of the spirit of architecture.

Chapter 9, devoted to a development of 'the inside and the outside', is probably the most helpful discussion of Venturi's intentions in architecture and urban form. He opens by quoting from E. W. Sinnott: 'The external configuration is usually rather simple, but there is packed into the interior of an organism an amazing complexity of structures which have long been the delight of anatomists.'[10] For Venturi 'contrast between the inside and outside can be a major manifestation of contradiction in architecture' and he attacks the twentieth-century orthodoxy of 'the necessity for continuity between them'. He points out that the Renaissance church already had this continuity in terms of the architectural vocabulary used both inside and out and as a consequence there is 'subtle modification but little contrast and no surprise'. The concept of 'flowing space', by which the distinction between 'inside' and 'outside' is dissolved, occurs in De Stijl and Mies van der Rohe's Barcelona Pavilion and also comes under attack. 'The essential purpose of the interiors of buildings is to enclose rather than direct space, and to separate the inside from the outside.' He quotes Louis Kahn: 'A building is a harboring thing.' In other words transparency of the glass wall, the 'dissolve' of distinctions between inside and outside, is too simplistic to allow for complexity and contradiction. The tensions, for example, in the clinging dress on a shapely woman are no longer exciting if at the same time one is fully aware of her underlying anatomy. This contrast between the exterior and the interior, this sense of secrecy and privacy is clearly central to the deep and most valuable of Venturi's contributions – his mysticism.

He opens chapter 10 with the statement: 'An architecture of complexity and accommodation does not forsake the whole. In fact I have referred to a special obligation towards the whole because the whole is difficult to achieve. And I have emphasised the goal of unity rather than of simplification in an art "whose . . . truth (is) in its totality".' Nevertheless it is in the interior organization of Venturi's buildings that we find the tension of complexity and contradition. The 'external configuration' is not usually simple, but rather exhibits too much of the 'contradiction juxtaposed', conflicting wave patterns rather than a surface tension. In other words the complexity and contradition are already visible on the external surface of the building, providing exactly what Venturi wishes to avoid, i.e. 'subtle modification but little contrast and no surprise'. If the design of a radio cabinet allowed the electronic circuits to spill out onto the control panel there would be confusion when one scanned the wavebands.

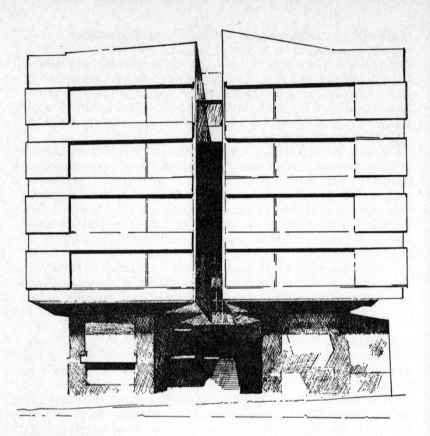

Apartment block, Rome.

It seems this way with Venturi's exteriors, even allowing a search for
'meaning in the complexities and contradictions of our own time'.

Of the examples of his own work shown in the last section of the book
there are two which most convincingly demonstrate Venturi's response to
complex stimuli. In the projected layout of Copley Square the desire lines
of pedestrian movement are subtly shifted just off course so that one
arrives not on an axis but beside it, a statement completely in the spirit of
Tintoretto. The Franklin Delano Roosevelt Memorial project conceived
'an open space' which linked the existing monuments around the periphery
of the site and therefore draws its own existence from an existing
complexity. Both examples avoid the contradiction of 'either/or' which
inevitably comes into play in the problem of relating a new statement to an
existing one. The exploitation of existing complexities and contradictions,
the inclination to accommodate, to include rather than complement,
characterizes both projects. One is reminded of the relationship between a
Mozart concerto and the performer's own cadenza: in playing variations on

the existing themes Venturi highlights the 'hidden order' without disrupting the whole.

Perhaps in the last analysis one must heed what Venturi says rather than merely attempt to rationalize what he does, and that is surely the value of *Complexity and Contradiction*. It provides an antidote to all the simple theories of design and design education which we tend to substitute for a deep search into the nature and mysteries of the real thing.

Intention and response

In the practice of architecture, as in the practice of all the other arts, there are the twin components of 'intention' and 'response'. In a building, as in any other work of art, the architect must have a thesis which he wishes to demonstrate or elaborate. The problem with architecture lies in its apparent actuality. By this I mean that whereas a poem or a picture is a framework of the artist's experience which is offered (abstractly through the medium of poetry or painting) to the reader or viewer as a framework for interpretation of his own or the artist's experience, the building-user mostly assumes that a work of architecture IS; in other words, a 'statement' has been made in which he is not necessarily involved.

By definition the building-user must be more interested in the function of architecture than in the 'intention' of the architect. Architecture suffers therefore from this apparent 'actuality' because its abstract qualities are valued, and would appear to be increasingly so valued, less highly than those qualities which we have come to describe as 'building performance'. Yet if we carry this preoccupation with the measurement of performance to its logical conclusion we must ultimately deny that architecture has 'delight', since only commodity and firmness can be so measured. This would in turn lead us to the conclusion that 'abstraction' had no part to play in the realization of 'environments'; in other words if all is measurable in terms of environmental performance then the 'intention' and 'communication' have no part to play in the realization of architecture. We should also have to question whether architecture is an art, whether it is capable of expression or the stimulation of responses within the complex frameworks of experience and the imagination, or merely a factual solution to a performance specification, i.e. a technical skill.

As Tatarkiewicz has pointed out,[1] the concept of art has in the past been fixed in theory while remaining rather fluid in practice. Whereas the ancients tended to despise the 'common' arts which required physical effort and to elevate the 'liberal' ones which did not, the Middle Ages upgraded the 'common' arts by calling them 'mechanical'. But 'art' continued to mean the liberal arts and even Leonardo da Vinci distinguished between the art of painting and the 'mechanical' art of sculpture. It is not until towards the end of the seventeenth century that a realignment takes place, with music and literature moving into the higher category, while it was realized that logic and arithmetic really belonged to the sciences. In this way, says Tatarkiewicz, the modern concept of 'arts' came about, no longer including what used to be called mechanical arts (these are now crafts not arts), nor the one-time liberal arts which turned out to be sciences not arts. What remained was only the visual arts, music, literature, and the theatre. It can be seen that, throughout these changes in the definition of the 'arts', architecture as *conceived* could be designated as a liberal art, simply because the basis of design is theoretical and mathematical and without physical effort, whilst architecture as *executed* remained as a common or mechanical art, or more recently a craft. Furthermore, although the category of non-arts, i.e. sciences, became clearer in concept, the difficulty of relating the visual arts, music, literature and theatre within the category 'arts' was the difficulty of determining what these different activities had in common. It was not sufficient, says Tatarkiewicz, to describe the 'arts' as the realm of ideas, or as being commemorative of people and/or events, or as being metaphorical in content. It was not until 1747 that a widely accepted answer to the question was provided by the French aesthetician Charles Batteaux in his treatise *Les Beaux-Arts reduits a un même principe*. Batteaux's suggestion was that all the arts sought, in different ways, to imitate nature, going on to explain that this imitation was achieved by selecting from nature that which was beautiful, thus his category of '*les beaux-arts*'. This category, according to Batteaux, had seven divisions: painting, sculpture, architecture, music, poetry, oratory and dance. It is this definition of the 'fine arts', i.e. that their common denominator was *beauty*, that was well established by the time that Victoria came to the English throne. In other words, art, as defined in Lalande's philosophical dictionary, is '*le production de beauté*'.

So for Batteaux the production of beauty meant the imitation of nature's beauty, suggesting that all art had an original source or 'first cause'. In his *Essai sur la Peinture* of 1766 Diderot put his own view more demonstratively,[2] calling for sentiment, surprise, terror, outrage, 'then, after that, delight my eyes if you can'. Yet as Anita Brookner has reminded us[3] Winckelmann's basis for the Neoclassical was a false-*naïf* ideal imitation of the ancients, or an imitation of nature's imitators. Thus began the second-hand tradition of the *beaux-arts*. Diderot was interested not in the imitation of the Greek product but of the Greek spirit. In his *salon* of 1767 there is an outburst against the thoughtless imitation of the antique, in which, without mentioning Winckelmann, he completely demolishes the German's theory of the '*beau ideal*' on historical grounds. How did the Greeks form their style when they had no antique form from which to copy? he asks. For the Greeks, after all, antiquity meant barbarism, savagery, an untamed state of nature. Instead, Diderot maintains, they copied their *modele idéal*, in other words they took from nature those elements which, if not already perfect, were seen to be perfectible. Perfectibility should therefore be the rule for the moderns as it was for the ancients. Imitation is a non-progressive act; perfection requires persistence in research and development; innovation alone is not enough.

Batteaux's 'selection of what is beautiful in nature' became to Diderot 'what is perfectible in nature', thus although Diderot like Winckelmann believed in the superiority of Greek art his explanation of this superiority was a purely materialistic one, i.e. given their climate and way of life the Greeks were able to discard the grosser deformities of nature and then put the principle of perfectibility into operation. The emphasis therefore shifted from the 'imitation' of selected (beautiful) elements, in Batteaux's thesis, to the 'improvement' of selected (perfectible) elements in Diderot's. Writing in the seventeenth century Fréart de Chambray[4] had already anticipated Diderot's concept of perfectibility by stating categorically that 'there is nothing worthwhile in the world which this divine country did not bring forth in all its excellence . . . the Greeks invented the arts which possibly were seen in their perfection in Greece alone'. Yet it was a speculative view of ancient Greece and what was thought to be Greek that had inspired de Chambray to write in this tone. The Sicilian temples of Agrigentum and Silenus were not visited in modern times by northern Europeans until 1725, and those of Paestum not until 1746 (Figs.21, 22). Also, it was not until 1751 that measured drawings of Paestum were taken to Paris, and published engravings of the Acropolis in Athens were not put on sale in London until the same year. In fact the monuments did not become widely known until the publication in 1758 of drawings of the Athenian monuments made by the French architect Leroy, although Jacob Spon's engraving of the Parthenon had appeared in 1678 and the engineers Plantier and Verneda had drawn views of the Acropolis during the Venetian bombardment of 1687. The early eighteenth century also saw the excavations of Paul Lucas, Tournefort, the Comte de Caylus and the Fourmonts, while the ruins of Athens were illustrated in Richard Pococke's *A description of the East and other countries*, Volume III, published in 1745, preceding Stuart and Revett by three years.

When the French Jesuit priest Marc-Antoine Laugier published his *Essai sur l'Architecture* anonymously in 1753 it is unlikely that he had any access to illustrations of Greek architecture and he had certainly not visited Greece, yet the *essai* constituted a demand for a return to the principles of Greek architecture.[5] In contrast to previous architectural theorists who had stipulated that the decorative elements of architecture should be employed to express an apparent solidity of form, Laugier demanded that they be employed so as to achieve an *actual* solidity. To Laugier the truth of architectural beauty was in the structural integrity of a building. His stipulation that 'the parts of an Order be the parts of the building itself' meant that a structure must be reduced to its basic members, with the strength of the column supporting the weight of the entablature, in other words a complete return to Greek rationalism. Yet when in 1769 Laugier finally had the shock of seeing Leroy's drawings of the Athenian monuments he denied that 'in the ruins of Greece there is one profile or one interesting architectural detail of which one could hope to make successful use in practice'. In the last analysis, therefore, Laugier's taste was formed more by Roman architecture and the French renaissance examples of the seventeenth century and for this reason he preferred the 'elegant simplicity' of the Ionic and the *grandeur sublime* of the Corinthian to the Doric which had, in his view, 'the simplest and least elegant of all capitals'. He criticised its entablature for its harshness, squareness, heaviness and dangerous projection of its cornice, commenting that: 'The eye is hurt . . . to see these large blocks of stone hurled into mid-air.' The conceptual or literary view of the Greek spirit and the Greek spirit as revealed by the Parthenon left a credibility gap in the French theorist's mind. Laugier was, it appears, seeking examples that could be emulated in the 'modern style' of the eighteenth century. He required that Greek architecture imitate the simplicity of nature, or in Diderot's terms the 'perfectible' elements of nature, whereas the Doric still represented 'the grosser deformities of nature'. Laugier's expectation of architecture did not allow him to accept the Doric as part of his architectural world; his response to it had been conditioned by his own architectural environment in eighteenth-century France.

Tatarkiewicz divides the history of European concepts of art into four broad periods. The first stretched from the fifth century B.C. up to the sixteenth century A.D., when art was understood as 'production governed by rules'; the second spanned roughly 1500–1750, being transitional, during which the 'arts' and 'sciences' were separated out and new theories of art evolved; from the middle of the eighteenth century until the end of the nineteenth the new concept of art as 'production of beauty', formulated by Batteaux, was accepted as widely as the pre-sixteenth century concept had been; the first half of the present century was a period of doubt concerning the validity of Batteaux's concept. We are now in a fifth period, which might be categorized as one of total uncertainty.

Most of Tatarkiewicz's attention is focused on the exclusivity or inclusivity of the term 'art', whether for example it is a skill or a product, a general or a particular description, whether Batteaux's restriction of seven *beaux-arts* still obtains in the face of new claimants, like the cinema; whether our decision to exclude or include an activity or a product should in any way be influenced by the intention of those engaged in the activity or production, and so on. He goes on to list six current definitions of the phenomenon 'art' in terms of its distinguishing features: (1) that it produces beauty; (2) that it represents or reproduces reality; (3) the creation of form; (4) expression; (5) that it produces aesthetic experience; and (6) that it produces shock. He points out that the list could be extended by including the definition of Ernst Cassirer (developed by Suzanne Langer) which says that art is, indeed, the creation of form, but of a special kind, namely forms which *symbolize* human emotions. He dismisses Diderot's concept of perfectibility as being more general than Batteaux's common denominator of beauty. Also he finds it peculiar to suggest that art is 'creativity without rules' because this contradicts the view of art held by the ancients: he suggests that this definition is too narrow as is the 'creation of illusions' put into Gorgias' mouth by Plato.

This leads us to the position where art may no longer be definable, or perhaps it would be better to say that it has never been definable, or in Tatarkiewicz's terms it has been fixed in theory while remaining fluid in practice. The continued need to define has, however, produced since 1950 the 'open' concept whereby, in the view of M. Wietz, 'It is impossible to propose any necessary and sufficient criteria of art; therefore, any theory of art is a logical impossibility, and not merely something difficult to achieve in practice . . . (as) artists can always create things that have never been created before; thus the conditions of art can never be laid down beforehand . . . (and) the basic assumption that art can be the subject of any realistic or true definition is false.'[6]

Nevertheless Tatarkiewicz proceeds to seek a valid current definition – 'for "art" is in fact a confluence of a number of concepts, and any true definition must take account of all of them'. It is here, I suggest, that we can understand the relevance of Venturi's open concept of including 'both–and' as a necessary conjunct of 'either–or'. Tatarkiewicz's aim, therefore, is to propose what he calls a 'disjunctive definition' of art. In other words, art has many forms and functions: it may stimulate, satisfy, move, impress or shock. It may aim for and achieve any one of these ends, i.e. the 'either–or', but surely the chances are that despite intention and form it will achieve a 'both–and' result in response.

Tatarkiewicz's conclusion is that: 'A definition of art must take into account both its intention and effect, and specify that both intention and effect may be of one kind or another.' Thus the definition, he proposes, will not only be a set of disjunctions, but will consist of two sets of disjunctions, and will run something like this:

'ART IS A CONSCIOUS HUMAN ACTIVITY OF EITHER REPRODUCING THINGS, OR CONSTRUCTING FORMS, OR EXPRESSING EXPERIENCES, IF THE PRODUCT OF THIS REPRODUCTION, CONSTRUCTION OF EXPRESSION IS CAPABLE OF EVOKING DELIGHT, OR EMOTION OR SHOCK.'

The *definition of a work of art* will not be very much different:

'A WORK OF ART IS EITHER A REPRODUCTION OF THINGS, OR A CONSTRUCTION OF FORMS . . . .'

Tatarkiewicz therefore gains in the open-ended inclusivity of 'either–or' within the definition, but has failed to appreciate the exclusivity of 'either–or' in that this alternative, or choice, only operates at best on the causal or intentional level, whereas to be inclusive on the effect or communicated level the activity or product may achieve a 'both–and' impact. So, the artist may intend only to shock but manages also to delight. In the time/taste scale of art appreciation what shocked Laugier in the Parthenon tends to fill us with a sense of awe. It certainly had that effect on Worringer. What appears 'either–or' to one observer may represent 'both–and' to another. In Clive Bell's view, for example, architecture would only qualify as 'art' if it were 'pure form': this would not unnaturally exclude most buildings purely on the grounds of their usefulness. Nevertheless a building user, unaware of either Tatarkiewicz's disjunctive definition of art *or* the architect's intention, may respond on one or more levels beyond his general satisfaction with the thermal, spatial, acoustic and light levels. He will do this involuntarily, responding in accordance with his intuitive, i.e. subconscious, assessment of the particular building or environment in relation to other buildings or environments that he has experienced either at first-hand or vicariously through a theoretical study of architectural intentions.

Responses to architecture and/or environments, to the arts in general, therefore, are conditioned by previous experience rather than one artist's intentions. If one's experience has been limited, then the response to experiences outside one's own are similarly limited on the first encounter with the new factors. In my own case I find that music of the post-Bartok era is beyond my response, principally because it is beyond my threshold of interest and therefore experience: similarly, Polish peasants in the Zakopane area of the Tatra mountains, brought up in wooden houses constructed entirely from large sections of logs and decorated inside by wood-carving within a frozen tradition, and having little or no experience of post-war town life, would not find a block of concrete flats sympathetic, however much better it may be for them in theory or by intention.

Responses, then, are conditioned by previous experience which in turn manifests itself in values and value judgements about the artefacts with which we are confronted. This is the fundamental difficulty of the architect. He must have intentions; he knows that these intentions may be only part of his personal language; yet to progress beyond established 'taste' he must deal in innovations. His territory is therefore the no-man's land between 'delight' and 'shock'. Without response, except to environmental measurables, his art can be no art. As Tom Stoppard puts it in his play *Jumpers*, 'if rationality were the criterion for things to exist the world would be one gigantic field of soya beans'.

Playing the environment cool

Clearly any discrepancy between 'intention' and 'response' can bring about a failure in communication in any art. Yet our inability to define the objects and qualities of art except in the broadest, most open-ended terms means that the very complexity and diversity of any art 'language', the vast range of sublety in both intention and expression, must allow for variety in understanding. In other words, in common with all other languages the art 'language' will be capable of being misunderstood as well. No living language can exclude this possibility. Only a dead language like Latin, i.e. one that is no longer in use and is therefore finite in its structure, vocabulary and form, can be absolutely described and understood by its rules.

The language of the Greek Doric as emulated in the Greek Revival is an example of this fixity of form and use in a dead language. But whilst it was a living language it was capable of variety in accent and stress, as is readily seen by comparing the Parthenon with the temples of Paestum (see page 81 and Fig.22). This suggests that, even when there are *rules of production*, there will be a 'high' style and other variations on it which we might describe as 'low'. It is the difference, in fact, between *Hochdeutsch* and the Austrian dialect, between BBC English and cockney or any regional English dialect. In attacking Marxist aesthetics as being 'in the main stream of the *bourgeois* and "high art" traditions', Phil Virden[1] accuses the logical positivists of omitting political and social structures in their programme of logical and linguistic analysis, adding that contemporary English philosophy 'refuses to admit that it is people who use language and logic, and it is people, not words or symbols, who mean things, and that people come in many varieties'.

Virden takes the work of Basil Bernstein as his basic reference, especially Bernstein's distinction between 'elaborate' and 'restricted' speech codes. In essence Bernstein's thesis is that speech and cognitive styles vary with modes of social relatedness. Bernstein says that some people have to survive situations of great complexity and change, operating at complex levels of symbolization and speaking in a complex and explicit manner in order that their meanings are unambiguously clear to the comparative strangers with whom they deal on a daily basis. This description would seem to fit the architect, who has to cope with an ever-increasing complexity of terms and concepts varying from the traditional 'architectonic, through the urbotectonic to the ecotectonic'.[2] Most people, however, lead more routine lives which are simpler in structure and as a consequence they do not have to anticipate the 'next move', nor do they have to make their intentions explicit because their immediate 'family' of acquaintances shares their own assumptions about how things 'are' or 'should be'.

The result is, says Bernstein, that some people are highly practised in elaborate thought and speech whilst others are not; and the power and authority hierarchies of industrial societies are therefore inclined to inhibit most people, most of the time, from thinking and speaking in novel and creative ways. In other words people are conditioned by their background environment, educational environment, all the *environments of experience* in fact, and these conditioning environments will limit or de-limit their social mobility in speech and action. They will also, of course, affect people's responses to works of art.

'Art languages' are a specialized form of communication; they convey information and/or 'messages' but the availability of this information – accessibility to the artist's intention – will vary. It will, in other words, be relative to the degree of 'highness' or 'lowness' of the art form. For example, ballroom dancing consists of technique rather than content, whereas in ballet the technique is subservient to the 'message' or symbolic content of the dance, and in Indian dance the 'message' is paramount with the technique entirely at the service of conveying, symbolically, the story which is being presented in dance form.

For this reason we must categorize ballroom dancing as a 'low' or 'popular' art, requiring minimum effort to understand what ballroom dances are about. In fact they are *about* nothing, being merely codified movements of the body in response to set musical patterns. They may provide a release from or contrast to normal routine life, in which the body is employed in other ways; they are simply pleasurable for those who enjoy them. This 'pleasure' content may be found in all folk art, whether it be dancing or decorative painting. The patterns are fixed, i.e. 'traditional', and the intention is 'understood' in advance; all that remains is that one should enjoy the movement, sound, colour, or whatever it is that is produced in the folk or popular art tradition.

European ballet and Indian dance must be categorized as 'high' art forms and their relative highness in the overall hierarchy must depend upon the expertness of one's knowledge about them and therefore ultimately upon one's 'point of view'. When we remember that architecture extends from functionalism, i.e. providing bare shelter, on the one hand, and the 'high art' of cultural symbolism on the other, we can begin to understand the difficulties of practising so open-ended an art and the virtual impossibility of explaining and justifying its purpose to those who take up extreme positions in the demands they make upon it. The pure formalism required by the Clive Bell school is hardly likely to make much impression on, say, the Housing Ministry in an overpopulated country where housing the whole population must take precedence over all other considerations. It is necessary to point out, however, that the functional requirements of today's economists, sociologists and five-year planners are subject to the same ephemeral effectiveness as those of art theorists, i.e. that which is imposed upon society rather than growing from within it is bound to be only a fad or fashion since it is not connected with the essential rituals of that society.

The current tendency to criticize architects for their failure to meet society's requirements presupposes that the clients and 'society' are one and the same, or that clients have the same high concern for society's requirements as is accorded the architect. Of course, it could be argued that the architect has brought this criticism upon himself precisely because society has never accorded him more than a subservient role in the shaping of the built environment and nobody would ever have suspected that he had more than a minor responsibility for this aspect of our affairs if he had not claimed otherwise. But, in fairness, his claims have only been aimed at clarifying the architect's role in an age when private patronage is in sharp decline and the danger of the total absorption of the building programme into consortia and 'package deals' is all too apparent. It is a fact that little contribution, in the long run, is made to environmental improvement or rehabilitation by mass building programmes. Amazingly, in Britain piecemeal developments of a very high standard do continue to come from the hands of a dwindling but increasingly conscientious and skilful band of architects. But in Polish Silesia, particularly at Katowice, where the mass housing programme has really got under way, twenty-storey slab blocks half a kilometer in length are not uncommon. In contrasting the two results it is easy to praise one group of architects while blaming the other, but it is important to remember that it is the political and economic system that 'makes' the architecture – at best the architect is *asked* to do such and such, more often than not he is required to comply with severe restrictions (leaving aside bye-laws and other universal hazards of practice), at worst he is *compelled*, *told* and *directed* to perform according to standards which are below his own *minima*.

It is worth recalling this double standard of performance when we assess the relative highness or lowness of a particular building on the architectural scale. One-hundred-and-sixty square feet of floor space in a concrete sandwich may not seem like much of a windfall to a Polish architectural historian and his wife, having to make their home there, but to the homeless such a possibility represents more than the mere *beauty* of high art, it is a miracle. This means that what we say about architectural language can only be presumed to have universal meaning in conditions which are universally equal. We must make our observations about the language of architecture, accepting discrepancies in patterns and standards as a necessary ingredient of comparison and therefore improvement.

We know that all language situations in general have a number of rules governing successful transmission and reception. For example, the sender and receiver must share the same language, that means they must be agreed on the symbolic code that is to be used. Then the sender and receiver must be agreed about the 'when', the 'how' and the 'why' of message-sending. Another important consideration is that the message should be capable of reception in spite of surrounding 'noise'. Virden points out that in the arts, even allowing the existence of the third condition, it is highly unlikely that the first two will be met. Except in a totalitarian society, where art like everything else is a matter for prescription, the artist and the public do not necessarily have the same expectations of art. Virden says: 'Meanings will always be read into messages, however, so it is quite possible for an artist and public to be linked by mutual misunderstanding, although the public will often think the artists are charlatans and the artist will think the public is philistine.'

The problem of architecture is a difficult one in the terms prescribed by Virden. He defines a work of art as a 'cultural artifact that exists to be contemplated in its own right' and says: 'This does not mean that works of art are purposeless, but that the practical question "What shall I do with it?" does not arise when we are confronted with one.' He goes on: 'In conveying messages about experience, art works also implicitly convey messages about the categories by which we experience. Again, and most importantly with art "the medium *is* the message". How else can we account for the fact that many people can react violently, with feelings of even physical nausea, towards alien art forms? . . . To acknowledge the legitimacy of an alien category system is to relativize one's own cosmology, to subvert the very assumptions of one's everyday existence.'

Virden asserts that only differentiated and literate cultures separate 'art' from 'life' and the aesthetic from the functional attitude, which means that literates are more conscious of the symbolic function of cultural objects and therefore use them as ritual surrogates. He points out that the 'messages' conveyed by art will require systematic variations in the forms of communication, and suggests that 'Bernstein's theory of linguistic and cognitive styles can be widened to become a theory of symbolic and cosmological styles in general. An elaborated linguistic code is and implies elaborate functioning in general. Thus, at least potentially, there will be consonance amongst a person's various modes of symbolic operation, such that an habitually complex mode of symbolic operation via one medium would facilitate and imply complex functioning via the other symbolic media.'

Virden argues that 'art language styles' should be analysable in principle, but in drawing attention to the difficulties, particularly in the case of poetry, he underlines the problems of so analysing architectural language. '. . . much elaborated code poetry conveys meanings in highly compressed forms – it is the form of a restricted variant of an elaborated code that is intelligible only to those who share many esoteric assumptions with the writer.'

In considering the total patterns to be analysed in architecture Virden lists 'space', 'form relationships', 'colour', 'texture', and 'function'. It is this last category, of course, which presents the greatest difficulty when taken in context with the others, for we certainly do have to ask of architecture 'What shall I do with it?'. But functional requirements, although specific in broad terms, permit considerable variation in details, so that like all 'contents' they will, as Virden says, 'vary and art will not perform the same function for all people and groups. Often the message only becomes apparent to the viewer if he closely shares the assumptions of the artist . . .'

This brings in the question of 'taste', since 'sharing assumptions' automatically presupposes similar conditioning, shared experiences and so on. It brings us back to Worringer's concept of empathetic response. Sharing assumptions means that a common wavelength exists, and all messages transmitted on that wavelength will be picked up by those who are tuned to it. 'To be' on the same wavelength as someone else means precisely that one has no difficulty in communicating with the other person because of shared experiences and therefore assumptions. Virden points out that 'with pure music the "content" *is* the form . . . Music, poetry, paintings and so on gain significance by being accompanied by messages through some or one other media.' This is surely the case with architecture, which can never be observed in isolation from the other media (or cultural frameworks) which establish the wavelength and control transmission and response. Yet the pattern of architectural education promotes its study in isolation from the overall cultural framework, providing about as much context of life and society as the medical student gets of sex and psychology, approximately two hours of each in a five-year academic course.

Thus although in architecture 'the medium' is 'the message' it depends more upon the support of the surrounding 'noise level' than the other arts. Precisely because buildings are used they are 'modified' by their users and the 'intentions' of architectural interiors are extended or filtered by use. Even a pure statement like Mies van der Rohe's Barcelona Pavilion changes when people are in it, yet there is not one single photograph showing the building 'in use'. A whole generation of architects and architectural photographers sought to abstract the art content from the life context. It is this abstraction which we have inherited in our training, and it therefore is an abstract 'message' (a highly elaborate code of symbols) which we tend to transmit in the buildings we design. In these conditions, with these cryptic messages, it is of course difficult to be socially and culturally relevant; the 'form' will not emanate from the 'ritual'.

The accessibility of the message in McLuhan's terms will depend upon

Mies van der Rohe's Tugendhat House at Brno, with people.

the relative 'hotness' or 'coldness' of the medium. He writes: 'There is a basic principle that distinguished a hot medium like radio from a cool one like the telephone, or a hot medium like the movie from a cool one like TV. A hot medium is one that extends one single *sense* in "high definition". High definition is the state of being well filled with data . . . speech is a cool medium of low definition, because so little is given and so much has to be filled in by the listener. On the other hand, hot media do not leave so much to be filled in or completed by the audience. Hot media are, therefore, low in participation, and cool media are high in participation or completion by the audience.'[3]

Clearly this places architecture in the category of cool media, with maximum participation in or completion of the message by the user, yet it has been the tendency of architects in our own society to assume that their architectural statements are finite ones, more or less immune from modification in use. Thus we have such statements, by architects in describing a church for example, as 'on entering the worshipper is immediately aware of (such and such a feeling) and senses the total (whatever it is) of the interior'. Of course, a church is a particularly difficult building to design in the twentieth century. Most Christian worshippers in the West received their first experience of churches in a Gothic or neo-Gothic example, where the *ethos* of building, ritual, music and vestments seemed consistently 'antique' and therefore authentic. People conditioned by such early and continuing experiences of churches will have a sense of 'churchness' which is not easily matched by a contemporary simulation of the original 'real thing'. The architect's task in church design, therefore, is not to attempt an imitation of an earlier Christian architectural spirit but rather to establish a background which allows the contemporary Christian to fill in the missing data with his own sense of the Christian spirit.

In design, reference to historical examples has the obvious hazard that it promotes sentimentality rather than a direct, uninhibited response of the senses. This cult of sentimentality has been inherited from the *Ecole des Beaux-Arts*: rules about how things *were* or *should be* constitute a wavelength interference in the process of discovering how things *are*. When there is too much historical noise-level we cannot hear the 'voices' of the present. The process of liberating primary and secondary school education from historical academic restraints is already in hand; the liberation of architectural education must be achieved if the cultural gap between designer and user, between art and life, is not to be widened. The basis of architecture is not the study of form in isolation, but a thorough understanding of ritual patterns on the one hand and the open-ended basis of technology on the other; form must emerge as the response of society's available techniques to its ritual needs, with the architect as catalyst.

The correlation of 'ritual' and 'form' in a society permits architectural 'statements' to be made. Thus, if there is an understanding of the concept 'church' or '*Rathaus*' then it is possible to express the essence of that concept in the design of the building. But a building in use is more than structure, form and colour; the added details of furnishings, paintings, particular ritual decorations, the very mode of life which is enacted in the building, all these things together interact to make the full architectural statement.

The danger of basing a study of architectural form on historical examples is that most of them can only be observed in their incomplete, i.e. unused, state. In this context indigenous architecture often provides more rewarding material since it shows the direct relationship of life-style to built form. The study of this direct relationship may help us determine our own ritual patterns in time to respond to them intelligently and perceptively. It is the underlying ritual patterns of our society that provide the key to formal intentions. Their study permits the anticipation of new needs, with new solutions which are required for problems that have no historical precedent.

The Victorians, for example, had to build railway stations when no concept of railway stations existed. What is essential in the appreciation of railway station form is the interaction that exists between trains, people and building, which can still be observed at the Lime Street terminal, Liverpool, and the through station at York. Both stations directly express in their form the non-static quality of railways. Unfortunately, stations not only displaced underprivileged communities, as at Somerstown for the construction of St Pancras, London but central city areas were permanently downgraded by the industrial character of railway business and its supporting services (Fig.23).

In the same way in our own century, roads, which were originally intended to allow space and free passage between buildings, have been given over to motor traffic and hence form an interference with human life rather than the promotion of it. Motor travel is an essential ritual of twentieth-century man and the motor car dominates the roads in our towns and cities. It is logical therefore to turn our backs on roads and railways, or better still to build a new environment over them. It is in accepting a new non-relationship to roads and railways that we can find new forms that are a logical response to our ritual pattern of mechanised nomadism. This is the level of design strategy that is necessary if we are to create significant forms in our own time. Yet we continue to cling to historical restraints imposed by traditional concepts of land patterns, with sites bounded by roads which have now been given over to the 'mechanical bride'.

The skyscraper is a direct product of restricted site conditions. High-rise offices have already gone beyond the boundaries of reason and usefulness, and high-rise housing has proved disastrous. Yet we hold on to the concept of high-rise because: (1) we imagine that it has something to do with the history of modern technology, and (2) we insist on maintaining historical street patterns with vehicular activities at the same level as pedestrian activity, when these street patterns have long since failed to meet the needs of the car. This clearly demonstrates our non-logical approach to the 'art' and 'cost-benefit' of environmental design.

Finally then, architecture is a cool medium: all environments require participation by the 'user'. Environmental memory, i.e. all previous experience, is a function of the mind; architecture, the physical enclosure, is either a constriction or an expansion of the environmental memory – it will allow the user to switch-on and participate or switch-off and opt out. Architecture is at best a framework for environmental experience; at worst it becomes a claustrophobic inhibitor, a rapidly outmoded container.

The architect as an open-ended system

Let us carry the discussion of 'form' and 'formalism', and 'style' and 'stylism' a little further. In the first place we cannot proceed very far with such a discussion unless we have an understanding of the form of our own society and its institutions. Our society, that is Western society as it is manifest in Europe and North America, is an open one. Sir Karl Popper recently summarized the characteristics of an open society as (1) '... free debate and especially debate about the wisdom or otherwise of government decisions', and (2) '... that institutions (within a society) should exist for the protection and freedom of the poor and weak.' He went on to point out that 'open societies are not very stable, precisely because they are exposed to critical discussion. Dictatorships are more stable, and so are utopias, which are always represented as static'. This suggests that the current debate about the purpose of architecture and the function of architects can only be a healthy indication of real interaction between environmental designers and those who inhabit their environments.

When a former editor of an architectural institute's journal describes that institute as ungovernable he is in fact striking a note of optimism about its future, although its future form must become, within the enlightened procedures of our open society, a matter for debate. One would be more alarmed, on the other hand, if the president of such an institute called for the support of members on the basis of loyalty to a collection of outmoded principles. The fact is that individual architects and an institute of architects form an interdependency, and how can anyone depend upon the support of an institution if the *modus operandi* of that body does not reflect the individual's commitments, values, and aspirations? To be a professional must mean the acceptance of a code of responsibility and one cannot be responsible without being involved. Clearly, there is a great deal of difference between playing a game and merely being a member of a supporters' club.[1]

Openness is stimulated in a society by encouraging flexibility of approach and adaptability in role-playing, trying to see other people's point of view whilst not compromising one's own standards or objectivity. The main purpose of the architect, the creation of environments, remains and will remain his true purpose. But in the past he has only been called up to perfume selected areas of the corpus, like an under-arm deodorant. Now the emphasis is upon health and beauty for the whole body, and that's a tall order. The formula is at best relative and at worst irrelevant. It is important in adapting to means to keep the end in view.

One hears the terms 'architectural determinism' and 'architectural paternalism', terms which suggest the image of the architect as one who precludes debate and freedom of choice, that he considers himself by virtue of his expertise and experience to be in a position where he can make decisions without reference to others, without taking their counsel. Sometimes architects have been in this position, but it is the exception rather than the rule. In the world of design what is sought after is a designer's sense of style – you could also call it flair or 'taste' – that thing which sets him apart from his fellow men, his ability to organize the fabric of life or at least a bit of it. But today most architects design for a committee, they have to match a brief that is often of the utmost complexity and, added to this, we now have the realization that there is no longer any single guiding principle or philosophy at work in our society at any one time – unless it is the principle of the 'fast buck' – no one system which can make sense, universal sense, of all the variables which must be catered for, all the options that must be kept open. A less resilient profession would have given up long ago.

We have all heard that the definition of a camel is a horse designed by a committee, yet the architect has at least tried to accept the challenge and although, unlike the surgeon, he cannot bury his mistakes, the architect has been more than a willing collaborator in the pathology of his work and role in society. The fact is that on the whole he is badly paid considering the responsibility he bears. He is much worse off than his engineer and quantity surveyor colleagues from the financial point of view, and he knows that only in the most arid and repetitive commercial structures can a decent profit margin be made on the fees he receives. Yet his critics wonder why he doesn't invest his overdraft in giving his buildings a periodic physical and 'psychiatric' examination. When the right level of investment is made in a building and the architect is not constantly asked to cut corners – as no aircraft or Rolls-Royce designer would be asked to do – the product almost invariably stands the test of time and idle gossip. It is important, therefore, for the briefing committee to realize that it now sits on the same side of the table as the architect.

Of course, if we are to believe our politicians and the newspapers, society would like to rid itself of these specialists it has brought into being. Yet, as Professor Kermode points out,[2] we cannot, as civilized beings, tolerate brute, inchoate, discrete 'reality' and we have a human need to make sense of it through intellectual schemes or paradigms. It is, of course, a question of what we mean by 'reality' and 'sense', and I have already ventilated some of the philosophical difficulties of determinism on pages 77–83. Kermode reminds us that all such schemes distort or misrepresent reality and to that extent are 'fictions'. He says that some fictions are more plausible than others; and that most need revising from time to time. His views would seem to have a general relevance in the fields of art and design. He reminds us that there is an increasing suspicion of the paradigms which 'fictions' impose upon reality. But the paradigms persist, he suggests, because they appear to be a necessary condition of human thought, and in matters of art and design they are another way of describing form.

I believe that the architect will survive because no other professional is trained to think about environments in a three-dimensional, formal way. It is the architect who offers the paradigm wherever environmental development and speculation exists. He it is who invents the 'fiction' which can replace the reality of existing environmental inadequacies and abuses. Under pressure from citizens' conciliar movements, which have come into being partly in response to the promises of the Skeffington Report[3] and partly in the general context of *vigilante* groups which are springing up throughout the Western world to protect property, privacy and established communities, those who govern and those who control land-use will increasingly have to demonstrate by convincing 'paradigm' and imaginative 'fictions' that what they propose accepts the principle that 'every generation of men, and therefore also the living, have a claim ... not to be made unhappy, where it can be avoided'.[4]

If it is the architect alone who can provide these convincing paradigms and imaginative fictions, the question remains 'Under whose aegis will he operate?'. The present trend shows that changes in client structure and administrative procedures have meant that in Great Britain more and more architects find employment in central and local government agencies with a parallel decline in private practice. There is a suggestion that productivity in central and local government practice is not related to man-hours and salaries paid. The simple fact that there is no fee structure against which to measure performance obviously contributes to a relaxation of pressure in central and local government offices: this often results in concentrations of older employees who are within the lower salary brackets because these men have been passed over by younger and more ambitious graduates. It is also a fact, however, that lack of ambition is not necessarily equivalent to incompetence and some architects are content to stay on the lower-paid rungs of the ladder because they wish to be closer to the building process than to administration. More equality of reward for all architects must be a priority. Only by such equality can the number and proper employment of architects be determined.

There are many who feel that central and local government practice has been enlarged out of all proportion to needs, with a resultant loss of objectivity and building quality. Many local authorities still depend upon private practices for substantial parts of their building programme, thus bifurcating skills and roles whilst not clarifying the task. Of course there must be Government involvement in research and development, i.e. the provision of pace-setters and standards to which the practitioner must conform. Under present arrangements in Britain there is naturally confusion resulting from Government involvement in research, development and executant roles. If there were obligatory Government standards for the measurement of competence it might then be possible to initiate independent research and testing establishments within the building industry whose prime purpose would be to identify and encourage excellence. As it is architects tend to offset gaps in competence by award schemes aimed at commending outstanding practice whereby the assessment of this supposed excellence is frequently based only on photographic or similar evidence and seldom has any relevance to building performance in use.

If I appear to have strayed a little from my topic I have done so merely because I believe that we cannot discuss the philosophy of architectural creativity if the architect himself does not have a comprehensible framework within which to operate. I believe that the architect has a role but like the role of his professional institute it needs redefining. Increasingly society has a need for men who not only shape our environments but care deeply and passionately about the strategies and tactics by which they are shaped. For this reason he no longer needs to pose, emulating more and more his ideal kind of client and becoming less and less like a realization of himself. Today the architect needs not only imagination and technical competence but also political skills, becoming a new type of *uomo universale*. Lateral thinking for the architect means thinking in terms of the whole team.

As my colleague at Liverpool, F. M. Jones, has pointed out, the full significance of the concept 'architect' has been given new credence by the whole engineering-electronic-media world, a fact manifested for example in the frequent advertisements for 'systems architects' and the employment of an architect to design, for example, the interior of the Concorde superjet.

The traditional role of the architect may be disappearing or in decline, but all traditions pass or are merged into new 'fictions' built upon new realities.[5] Old paradigms outlive their usefulness. If it had not been so the 'architect' (master mason) would have given way to the package-dealer in the Middle Ages. 'Does the aesthete who extols the greatness of the past as an argument against modern art have any idea how pallid his own response to, say, the Virgin of Chartres appears beside the mediaeval man's response? Or that his own aestheticism, however cultured, is in fact a form of sentimentality – since sentimentality at bottom is nothing but false feeling, feeling that is untrue to its object, whether by being excessive or watered down?'[6]

Old building forms and old roles have become collectors' pieces. Some of our cities themselves have become museums into which we are attempting to breathe the 'resonance of life'. Finite forms, which were not only comprehensible to our ancestors, even our immediate forebears, but highly desirable, have lost their function and therefore their significance. There was a time when it was possible to begin one's architectural training and have a fairly clear idea of what awaited one, as a qualified architect, at the end of the process. That certainty was still possible when I began my own training only a quarter of a century ago, or at least the uncertainty, the open-endedness of the professional role, was not as evident as it has been for the past decade. When in the late forties the Hunstanton school competition was launched I had just begun my pupilage but I was allowed to work on it because, having just left school, I was considered close to the problem. The conditions specifically stated that courtyard solutions would not be accepted and my master produced a scheme that 'fingered' about the site. To our surprise and outrage the Smithsons won with a courtyard scheme. In fact we should have been more outraged by the suggestion that the building form could have been prescribed in the first place.

Today the architect is himself rather like the modern work of art: 'No beginning, middle, end – such is the structureless structure that some modern literary works struggle toward; and analogously in painting, no clearly demarcated foreground, middleground and background. To the traditionalist, immersed in the classical Western tradition, all this will appear negative, purely destructive.'[7]

In other words, an open society (i.e. Britain under any Government other than a Communist or a Fascist one) is one that does not have totalitarian prescriptions about myths to be cultivated and roles to be played. The architect himself survives by becoming an open-ended system with reference to the environmental game.

Within the central tradition that runs from Aristotle through Thomas Aquinas into the very beginnings of the modern period man has sought the intelligibility of all Being, believing that the cosmos is, after all, intelligible. The beginnings of architecture as a unified profession in the eighteenth century were built upon the tenets of this central tradition. It was for this reason, in the Age of Reason, that classical forms really took root in the Neoclassical movement, and as a consequence the evolution of architecture suffered a further setback. The reason and formalism of classical antiquity were the backdrop to technological innovation, with Romanticism appearing as the antidote. In the face of the Industrial and later the Transport Revolution came an intense interest in classical archaeology, with the intellectual and cultural interests of society remote from the frontiers of technological innovation. It was in this way that the architect romanticized his role, becoming remote from the 'new realities', settling instead into an essentially conservative and reactionary position in society. The academies only served to harden the distinction between art as a classical and regulated concept and the 'new realities' of industrial technology and post-industrial blight.

It is not surprising, therefore, that the Western architect, who is now more aware of society (rather than a number of isolated individuals) as his client has found his own inherited classical vocabulary unconvincing and intolerable. He has experienced a profound change in his attitude towards society and in society's attitude towards him, and these transformations have confused him *pro tem*. But these changes are themselves part of the 'new realities' and as they have defied conceptual expression, and therefore solution, for the past two centuries, we must not be surprised if we have not managed to formalize the situation in the quarter of a century that has elapsed since the end of the last war. The reason is not hard to find; as Barrett says: 'The final intelligibility of the world is no longer accepted. Our existence, as we know it, is no longer transparent and understandable by reason, bound together into a tight, coherent structure.'

Hence the architect is the paradigm of modern man, as described by Max Scheler, thoroughly and completely problematic to himself, obsessed (as is existential philosophy) by the alienation and strangeness of man in his world, by the contingency of human existence, by the central and overwhelming reality of time for man who has lost his anchorage in the eternal.

Rules are no longer valid in terms of ends, i.e. solutions, but we have the technological means as well as guidelines for their employment. Culturally hallmarked forms have become devalued by over-use. Our response to all formal stimuli is blunted by over-exposure, especially if most of the examples are not the 'real thing', i.e. do not have 'the resonance of life', but are merely sentimental simulations of the original, and bad copies at that.

Our hope, therefore, lies not in systematic, rationalistic, conclusive efforts at perfection, but in the unsure, ambitious and even outrageous attempts to underline the open-ended nature of our being and of what we as architects are about.

I think that James Stirling does this when he takes the hothouse aesthetic from Paxton and tempers it with the environmental engineering that the intervening century has produced. His History Faculty building for Cambridge University is an open-ended building from the start, in planning, form, and therefore in association, but it is also original and inimitable in its environmental statement. And because it mocks the idea of an art gallery as a sacred cow of Western culture, I find the entry for the Burrell Collection Gallery Competition by Bryant and Mason a worthy example of the anti-academic investigation of the being or ISness of architecture, completely existential in its attack on the 'bad faith' of architectural formalism. The visualization of one of our society's central cultural symbols as a giant 'Ovaltine' advertisement set in the gently undulating landscape disputes with healthy open-endedness Gertrude Stein's definitive contention that: A rose is a rose is a rose.

'Architecture is what it wants to be', as Kahn has suggested, but its identity must inevitably come from those who make and use it. We endow it with our own associations, our own environmental memories or fictions.

Of all the London districts the name of 'Elephant and Castle' holds most promise of the exotic.[8] What a disappointment that there has never been a memorial to our fantasies. Surely the London Passenger Transport Board, faced with the challenge of providing a new electricity sub-station, could have done better than the exquisite but cryptic aluminium box (Figs.24, 25). The elephant folly designed for Louis XIV would have given flesh to the myth. Based on this I have made my own proposal for the site, including a fully castellated sub-station in the best public works tradition. As it is we are left with no alternative but to reinforce a new legend that the aluminium box in fact represents an 'Elephant in a Parcel'.

Purism in this context is merely another name for Puritanism. Both have the same effect, squeezing out our sense of fun with their straightlacing. An environment without wit and humour is no environment for Man.

Edwin Lutyens must be straining to get back to his drawing board. There seems to be more and more need for his inventiveness. Instead of taking ourselves so seriously we should be praying for his early reincarnation. His genius for inversion would be most helpful in determining new roles and profiles.

Contexts for the future of architecture

Style for primitive man consisted of survival by adaptation. Failure to adapt meant failure to survive. The alternative to personal adaptation was to vary the environment by moving from place to place. When no part of the earth's surface supported more than a small population it was possible to adopt nomadic habits and leave very little trace of one's movements. There were no roads or sewers or other arterial systems; every activity was swallowed by obliging nature. The surface of the earth remained largely undisturbed so long as nature maintained her grip on Man's freedom of choice. To settle, to give up the joys and hazards of the nomadic life, meant to conquer nature and suppress the natural system.

Civilization, the culture of settlements and cities, brought with it the concept of permanent structures, fixed lines of communication and trade, the security of knowing where you are in relation to somewhere else. It meant also the erosion of the earth's surface. Also, as the supply lines were extended and expanded over the past five-hundred years, what were formerly discreet veins have erupted into varicose disfigurations. Today, the land surface of civilized countries resembles the skin of a man that has been torn by broken blood vessels and ruptured organs. What was formerly the planned containment of nature for the benefit of settlement has become, in response to Man's conflicting supply lines, a gigantic overgrowth which is covering the earth and destroying the agents of natural balance. In seeking structural innovations for the remaining two decades of this century the performance specification which must be applied is the controlled balance of nature; the objective is a return to 'the Garden of Eden', with the restoration of Man's full enjoyment of ordered nature. In this sense innovation of built-form must be seen as the key to environmental engineering.

An ideal solution to the problems of land use might be achieved if: (1) all services, transportation, and industries were put underground; and (2) with the removal of surface transport networks land was removed from the artificial constraints of site boundaries. Conservation as we mostly understand it is merely the strict preservation of existing situations, protective maintenance of the *status quo* rather than creative restructuring. The removal of existing site boundaries would allow the re-allocation of land resources which are presently inhibited by established land-use patterns. The possibility of achieving land-use rotation (like Townsend's crop-rotation) would be opened up. In the long term the benefit would justify the cost but it is unlikely that money will be made available for such advances until there are also sweeping innovations in politics. Modern man wishes to be a nomad once more but the political institutions of his civilization inhibit him. His democracy is a freedom of no-choice.

The principle can still be applied, however, by rehabilitating the vast tracts of urban land that have been down-graded as a consequence of siting train terminals, for example, in city centres during the last century. The reclamation of this land has become one of our main objectives in the process of piecemeal engineering. Wilem Frischmann and I have described our proposals for rafting over large central urban wastelands in our paper 'Dual use of land in central urban areas'.[1] This method would allow the creation of new central parkland areas, restoring pedestrian-only access to buildings and open space at the new 'ground' level. A small example of the potential of this form of environmental engineering is provided by the opportunity of extending the present limits of Regent's Park, London, in an easterly direction, along the northern boundary of the present Euston Road, to allow a continuous parkland through to include King's Cross and perhaps The Angel, providing a new residential neighbourhood of some 50,000 bed spaces, with a scale and character say of Lincoln's Inn Fields.

This strategy of rafting over industrial sites and service areas would permit the extension of rehabilitation along all the major transportation lines throughout the country, concentrating residential areas with their shopping and educational facilities on the slopes of these newly created 'hills'. Developments above 'ground' would be entirely free of the noise and interference of transport and service traffic beneath. The result would be the release of land (which is presently being inefficiently used for building) to be devoted to agriculture and recreation. This would appear to be an obvious strategy for Great Britain, where the population density is currently 600 persons per acre and rising.

Unlike tunnelling this operation can be carried out with relatively little interference to existing services at ground level and has the overall advantage of concentrating the built environment along the principal lines of communication and supply. With the increased speed of trains this would make the advantages of London's Underground system available to the whole country. It would have the further benefit of eliminating train noise transmission in residential areas while completely removing the environmental down-grading currently associated with land adjacent to railways and highways. Travelling time would be shortened by increased speed so that the lack of view except from bridges would be of less consequence. Large-screen TV viewing lounges would allow passengers to watch the surrounding landscape or receive other information and entertainments.

This solution for land reclamation and rehabilitation is appropriate in highly populated small industrial nations, for example Japan and Holland. It is based on fixed or rooted facilities fed by high-speed mobile services. In this respect it is unlike mobile systems of urban and related containment such as those proposed by Cedric Price in his *Potteries Thinkbelt* (1965–6) and the 'Strip City' concept for the United States proposed by New York architects Craig Hodgetts and Lester Walker.[2] 'Strip City' is in fact a 200-mile an hour travelling city, poised over slower vehicular-lanes from which it absorbs slower travelling 'commuters'. Both concepts seem particularly appropriate for countries with great open plains between existing urban nodes, e.g. Russia, China and Australia. It is interesting to compare both these projects with Hans Hollein's model for a continuous city.

Rafting allows short-span support of the superstructure where a high incidence of support at ground level is not a disadvantage, but as continuous urban complexes will require vertical service shafts an alternative system of suspended superstructures may come into being, whereby the new developments would be hung rather than propped up. It would be a realization of 'hanging gardens'. The vertical support shafts, carrying both the lateral and transverse 'bridges', could be widely spaced and allow completely unimpeded movement of traffic at ground and underground levels. It would produce in effect a three-dimensional extension of the principle observed in the Ponte Vecchio, Florence, with multi-level use within a zone spanning from about 100 feet below ground to another 100 feet above, providing a nation-wide network of the 'boulevard city' system as proposed by Werweka for Paris.[3]

What is important in all the above concepts is the acceptance of mobility as an essential feature of the structure; either the structures themselves are mobile or concentrated movement patterns occur within them. In other words the structure exists in time as well as space; man is not moving from place to place by going from structure to structure, he is moving within structure: structure becomes the man-made environment rather than a mere interruption of the natural environment which we have inherited.

Renzo Piano has said: 'The structural revolution has moved, to my mind, in three primary directions; towards the space frame, the shell and the tensile structure.'[4] This statement contains a characteristically traditional limitation of the concept 'structure', with minimum attention to the systems approach. These outlines for the techniques of linear environments are, of course, dependent upon the concepts of space frame and tensile structures in their broadest sense. Structure here means 'form', whether the manifestation of that form is ectoskeletal or endoskeletal. Air walls, for instance, are invisible; they enclose without apparent form. Unlike inflatables they do not even manifest the concept 'support'. They

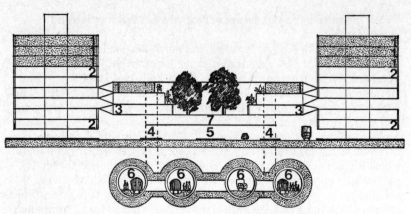

1 Housing	5 Service traffic
2 Offices, department stores, etc.	6 Existing underground transportation (or
3 Cafés, shops	motorway tunnels)
4 Vertical passenger links	7 Service level

Schematic section of Werweka's Boulevard City concept.

merely constitute a barrier between two environments, the included and the excluded. Clearly, in considering future building developments we can no longer confine our attention to concepts limited by the conventional reference to statics. Material strength like energy is relative to whether or not it is 'in use'. Future buildings will depend more and more on the balance of forces and energies that constitute the inclusion of the internal environment and the exclusion of the external.

Structure, therefore, must mean not only 'form' but also 'system'. In this sense it will be a continuation of the traditional conventions of structure, precisely because no form exists without a system which brings it into being. Formalistic substitutes for systems fall outside my context here. In building innovations the 'style' will come only in the life patterns which they promote and support.

Systems are the product of and the expression of prevailing technologies. We are no longer limited by our inherited building technology but we should be guided by it. Technology now includes all the systems, whether material or mechanical, that can be harnessed to environmental problem-solving. The sources of new structural systems will be found in balloon and rubber technology, tunnelling, submarines, and manned space-flight, in fact in everything from zip-fasteners[5] to vacuum-sealing. Even rock blasting becomes a constructive, as well as destructive, technology, as it provides an instant solution to the hole-in-the-ground type of problem.

We must review that concept of 'structure' which includes not only supporting but also enclosing systems. In the origins of man-made structures, in the most fundamental structural forms, there is no distinction made between 'support' and 'enclosure'. The eskimo's use of the shaped block of ice in the construction of his igloo provides a paradigm of this cohesive view of structure. Tents of the Ajdir Plateau in the Middle Atlas, the bamboo vaulting found in the Gulf of New Guinea, the *fragmites communis* parabolic arches of the Lower Tigris, the mud-brick vaulting found in *caravanserai* at Qum near Teheran, the fine clay-brick vaults in the Masjid-e-Jameh at Isfahan, the portable thatch roofs of Guinea, canvas awnings which become the roofs of streets in Sevilia, the underground courtyard housing found in the Chinese loess belt in the provinces of Honan, Shansi, Shensi and Kansu (which can be compared with the conversion of underground burial vaults into dwellings at Siwa in Egypt), the adaptation of the baobab (*Adansonia digitata*) tree of tropical Africa, the hollowing out by monks of the tufa chimneys in the Göreme Valley of Cappadocia – all these may be quoted as evidence of the inclusive support-enclosure tradition which dominates the evolution of structures in the man-made environment.

Architecture is merely an off-shoot of the evolutionary pattern of settlements: it has embroidered the fundamental tradition of structure by establishing the convention that allows the 'support' and the 'enclosing envelope' to be considered as two separate entities. The concept of architecture which is now most widely accepted has derived from this schism of 'science' and 'art'. Inflatable membrane structures, where the traditional concepts of floor, wall and roof become redundant, are a useful example of recent developments in the evolution of structure because they enable us to break with the convention that has been imposed on the building process by architectural prescriptions. Cedric Price and Frank Newby have also shown that the hole-in-the-ground enclosures not unlike those of the Chinese loess belt have a future as well as a past.

Generally speaking, therefore, a re-ordering of hierarchies in the archaeology of structures, a resifting of the evidence of other cultures (i.e. not only civilizations which, in seeking stability, symbolism and permanent 'style', must inevitably concentrate on enrichment rather than innovation), particularly nomadic cultures with whom we shall increasingly have common interests and objectives, is essential to the understanding of our own future steps in the evolutionary process.

My own view of the immediate future of structural innovation would be incomplete without 'tubes'. It is the tube that allows the most efficient containment of services, restoring the earth's surface to Man. Underground tubes have long been a part of our environment in the West and now the projected road/rail link between Italy and Sicily across the Straits of Messina will provide an example of underwater tubes, which, unlike the normal submerged tube projects, will float from moorings on the sea-bed.[6] The interesting fact here is that it has been found more flexible both in construction and operation to allow a separate tube for each road or rail traffic lane, so that the link will be made up of a total of eight tubes. This project opens the way for further research and development in the field of underwater tubes as transport/service links.

The projected Channel Tunnel is another example of this form of development. A proposal for the tunnel project by Professor Baker of Imperial College provides for a series of wide 'U's acting as submerged tubes between artificial islands, the islands facilitating ventilation. This proposal provides the paradigm for a system of habitable artificial islands to be built along the length of long-distance water tube links. We already have the complex artificial islands necessary for Atlantic oil-drilling rigs and the same principle could be developed for larger 'islands'. Also, there is the possibility of constructing floating islands, which could be moored to the ocean bed. An example of such islands is provided by Harris and Sunderland's proposal for the Thames Estuary, where large concrete 'boxes' were to be filled with expanded polystyrene and moored to piles driven into the river bed.[7]

The use of underwater transit systems would be consistent with expanded sea trade and traffic. Islands or submarine colonies located

Aerial view of cave dwellings carved into the Chinese loess belt.

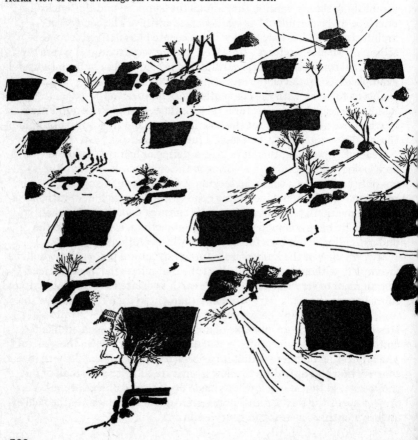

along these supply lines could themselves become depots for underwater farming and other resource-tapping activities. It would also be possible to use these submarine links to carry solar and other energy systems. Already experiments have been carried out in harnessing solar energy by floating inflatables above cloud level.[8] The environmental disadvantages of mass-scale air transportation are already sufficient to warrant the exploration of underwater intercontinental links which would provide a complete link-up of the world's resources. Having used space research to develop a satellite communications system would it not be appropriate to pool jet-engine and further space exploration funds for the development of underwater systems with the known advantages of submarine farming and the removal of existing airborne pollution sources.

The future of buildings must be sought in the areas where the natural balance of the environment must be adjusted or has to be restored. The emphasis will be on economy in the environmental system as a whole – the eco-system as we now call it – not merely in material terms but in relation to energy expended and conserved. The essential characteristic of our civilization is over-production and waste. Civilization is self-competitive, using more energy and resources than are necessary for operation and development.

Economic crises are crises of distribution and consumption. Over-production and waste consume the surplus on which civilization normally thrives.[9] Cost benefit should be concerned with identifying surplus before it exists: this potential surplus can then be anticipated in the design of the structure/energy complex. Structural innovation must contribute to our release from the straitjacket of conventional services: at the present time, structure, envelope, services and waste disposal are segregated. Structures of the future must provide not only support and enclosure, they must also integrate the energy system.

New sources of natural gas and oil are only temporary stopgaps in the total depletion of natural resources. Our real need is to tap the potential energy in our environment, or within reach of our planet, i.e. electrical, solar and so on. One of the objects of building innovation must be to harness potential energy and facilitate secondary production by recycling. In this way the 'moving' structure can be non-static but not anti-static, in fact activating static energy by the progress of its dynamic cycle.

New problems in the environmental sphere will provide the motivation to seek innovations. Clearly, the priorities are to be found in the areas of habitation, industrial processes, transportation and leisure. The highest incidence of mobility exists at the present time in transportation and industry, both areas notorious for their conspicuous consumption of energy, with no return to the national electricity grid for example. Commercial facilities and habitation are also heavy consumers of energy with no production in return. Most of the energy expended in human activity is lost permanently: sewage, for example, is a powerful source of potential energy. Our objective must be to obtain an energy yield within

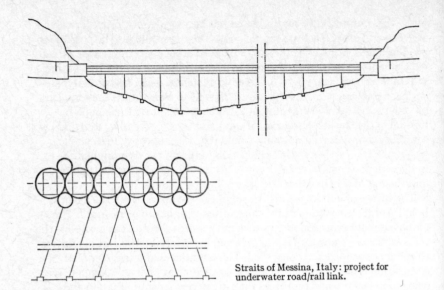

Straits of Messina, Italy: project for underwater road/rail link.

the structure of the built environment. When this energy yield is universally 'on tap' our mobility will be limited only by the kind of structures we are able to carry around and 'plug-in' to energy sources.

Thus the challenge exists on two levels: (1) in the basic support/energy/service structures which will become more and more essential to environmental balance and control, and (2) in the area of demountable, variable-form, mobile convenience/activity units, which will provide new patterns of environmental freedom in relation to what is built. Ironically, this could re-establish the separation of 'support' and 'enclosure' but the difference in its re-application is that the more permanent framework ('support' in the most general sense) will permit the interchange of service and convenience/activity units. The building will become more akin to the natural structure of the earth with the mobile/demountable units providing the variables. Architecture, far from being dead, will gain the flexibility of the organ keyboard and the neon sign. Churches which are used only once a week will be erected when they are needed: cathedrals will not need to remain empty for 300 days a year.[10] Both interior and exterior configurations will be capable of change. The main investment will be in the semi-permanent built-form which will be pure engineering. These built forms will provide a continuous network of supply lines, an overlay on Nature, which will restore Man's nomadic freedom.

We already have the potential for this freedom but we are committed to a pattern of conspicuous consumption which necessitates bifurcation in the expenditure of energy. Thus our vehicles, our personal mode of transport, carry their own energy systems in travelling between destinations. In this context, it is interesting to note that the new concept of 'Strip City' comes from the USA, where the simple convenience of the passenger train has been largely abolished. This underlies the desire for complex convenience in the New Nomadic Age. The tent, the ever-versatile structure, is the paradigm: its successors will provide the new mobile demountable environments.[11]

It will be in the full realization of Venturi's concept of building as 'both/and' rather than 'either/or' that the future of environmental construction will lie. A clear distinction between the semi-permanent aspects of pure engineering and the virtual do-it-yourself environmental kits of the type foreshadowed by, for example, the Archigram group, is essential before research and development in built-form can proceed. Without such a distinction we are in danger of confusing the purely temporary expedient of say the motorway with the semi-permanent form of an environmental structure like the city. Without a clear understanding of contexts we shall cling to the *status quo* and continue to dissipate our energies and resources without real advance.

1

2

1 Ronchamp: Notre-Dame du Mont
by Le Corbusier.
2 Dublin: New Library for Trinity
College by Ahrends Burton and Koralek.
3 London: Household Cavalry
Barracks, Hyde Park.

4 Marseilles: the first Unité d'Habitation.

5 Liverpool: Roscoe Hall of Residence, landscaped for the birds rather than the pedestrians.

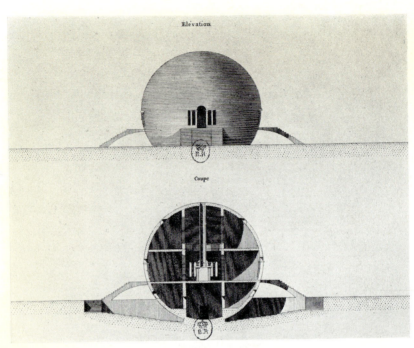

6 Claude Nicholas Ledoux: project for a guardhouse – pure geometry in the romantic landscape.

7 Serifos: the indigenous Greek island architecture with the church emphasized by a classical motif.

8 Richelieu: view of the town gate from the Cardinal's château.

7

8

9

10

II

9 Valletta: view across Grand Harbour.
10 Valletta: plan of the city in 1565.
11 Warsaw: the main square in the reconstructed Old Town.

12

13

12 London: Covent Garden Market
in 1973.
13 Albi: detail of the fortified cathedral.

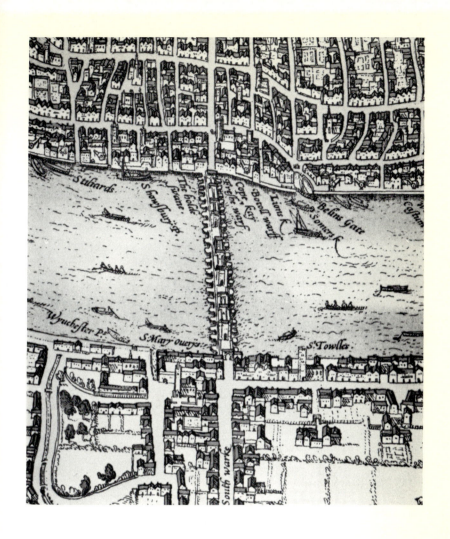

14 London: London Bridge, linking the City with Southwark.

15 London: Regent's Park Zoo, the Elephant and Rhinoceros House by Casson and Conder.

16 Berlin: Das Altes Museum by Schinkel.

16

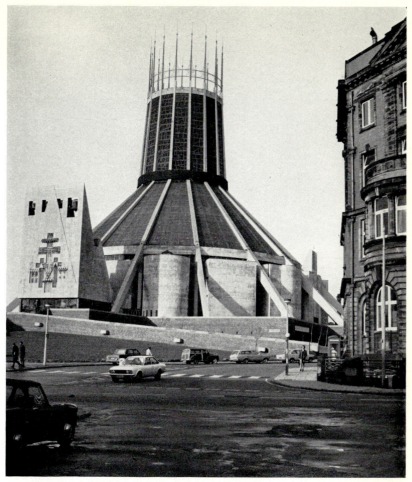

17 Liverpool: the Cathedral of Christ the King by Gibberd.

18 India: Graeco–Buddhist sculpture, second century A.D.

18

19 London: St George's Church, Bloomsbury by Hawksmoor.

20 London: Regent's Park semi-detached houses – symmetry becomes duality.

21

22

140

23

21 Agrigentum: Classical temple in the
Doric style.
22 Paestum: Archaic temple in the Doric
style.
23 London: St Pancras Station.

overleaf:
24 London: the Elephant and Castle before
the First World War, and
25 after post-World War II reconstruction.

24

25

Notes

Preface

1
Golo Mann: The History Lesson
Encounter, August 1972

2
Le Corbusier
If I had to teach you architecture
Focus 1938, London

3
Charles Jencks: Rhetoric and Architecture
Architectural Association Quarterly,
Summer 1972, pages 4–17

Architecture – man and myth

1
T. S. Eliot: *Selected Poems*
London 1954

2
G. S. Kirk: *Myth*
Cambridge 1970

3
Harold Osborne
Aesthetics and art history, an introduction
London 1968

5
Gjerløv-Knudsen
The Philosophy of Form
Copenhagen 1962

6
Mario Praz: *On Neoclassicism*
London 1969
'Eliot observes that Milton's original
sensuousness was withered early by book-
learning, that his language is artificial and
conventional, that in fact he writes English
like a dead language, that with him
everything is sacrificed to a musical effect,
so that poetry is sometimes debased to a
level of "a solemn game". We may be struck
by the similarity of these criticisms to those
which are usually aimed at neoclassical art.'
(see T. S. Eliot, 'Note on the verse of John
Milton' in *Essays and Studies by Members of
the English Association*, Oxford 1936)

In search of order

1
'Even a little knowledge of ethical theory
will suffice to convince you that all important
questions are so complicated, and the results
of any course of action are so difficult to
foresee, that certainty, or even probability,
is seldom, if ever, attainable. It follows at
once that the only justifiable attitude of
mind is suspense of judgment; and this
attitude, besides being peculiarly congenial
to the academic temperament, has the
advantage of being comparatively easy to
obtain. There remains the duty of persuading
others to be equally judicious, and to refrain
from plunging into reckless courses which
might lead them Heaven knows whither. At
this point the arguments for doing nothing
come in; for it is a mere theorist's paradox
that doing nothing has just as many
consequences as doing something. It is
obvious that inaction can have no
consequence at all.'
This is not a manifesto of the 1960s; it was
written by F. M. Cornford in his guide to the
young academic politician, *Micro-
cosmographia Academica*, published in 1908.

2
Christian Norberg-Schultz
Intentions in Architecture
London 1963

3
Paul Klee: Notebooks Vol.I: The thinking eye
London 1961

4
Anton Ehrenzweig: *The hidden order of art*
London 1967

5
Peter Brown: *The World of Late Antiquity*
London 1971

6
George Steiner
*Bluebeard's Castle: some notes towards a
redefinition of culture*
London 1971

The city and the politics of form

1
C. P. Cavafy in *Four Greek Poets*
London 1966

2
William Godwin
Enquiry Concerning Political Justice
London 1789 and 1796

3
John Millar
*The Effects of Commerce and Manufacturers,
and of Opulence and Civilisations, upon the
morals of a People*
London 1803

4
Adam Smith: *Wealth of Nations*
Ed. Cannan, London 1961

5
Karl Popper
The Open Society and its Enemies
London 1945

6
Marshall McLuhan
The Media fit the Battle of Jericho
1956

7
Serge Chermayeff and Christopher Alexander
Community and Privacy
New York 1963

8
Sir Peter Medawar: 'The Future of Man'
Reith Lectures: BBC, London 1959

9
'Man alive' programme BBC2 TV
London, May 1972

10
Howard Saalman: *Mediaeval Cities*
London 1965

Significant form in architecture

1
'The French speak of *Gestalt* psychology as
la psychologie de la forme. This translation is
meant to indicate that the *Gestalt* principle
is only indirectly concerned with the subject-
matter of natural things. To call a football
team or a painting or an electric circuit a
Gestalt is to describe a property of their
organization. *Gestalten* function as a whole,
which determine their parts. Four musicians
who form a string quartet will create a
unified style of performance. This style is a
delicate crystallization of affinities and
conflicts of temper. It is a balance of the
behaviour of each player.'
Rudolf Arnheim
Gestalt Psychology and artistic form
Aspects of form
London 1951

2
'. . . architecture is the art of enclosing space,
there are two basic elements: space, and the
material used to enclose it. For a work of art
to emerge from the process it is essential that
these two basic elements should be effective;
and it is not enough that the envelope
enclosing the space should be effective, the
art is in the effective synthesis of these two
elements. If this is accepted as an elementary
axiom, then we must conclude that classical
architecture never reached artistic perfection
– that it remained a lapidary art to be
judged by its external proportions, in other
words it was never decisively emancipated
from the sculptural complex in which it
originated. It is not until we come to the
Romanesque period that a sensibility for
space begins to swell the interior space to
some expressive purpose.'
Herbert Read: *The Origins of Form in Art*
London 1965

3
Lionel March and Steadman
The Geometry of Environment
London 1971

4
Barry Commoner: *The Closing Circle*
London 1972

When the elephants were white!

1
The Fra-Fra House
Architectural Design, June 1962, page 299

2
The Dingling, tomb of the Emperor Wan Li, near Peking, early seventeenth century, is another example of this plan form.

3
Architectural Design, November 1962

The environmental memory

1
This interview is more or less identical with that given to *The Paris Review* fifteen years earlier by Simenon.

Language and meaning

1
As I find the Cathedral of Christ the King a particularly useful example of what not to do I am always on the look out for those who find it a successful building. Recently a doctor told me: 'I find it an intriguing building. You see, it's so improbable from the outside that one simply has to go in and find out what it's about.'

2
See pages 101–108 for further discussion.

(Ad)Venturi(sm): pragmatism and/or empiricism?

1
David Jones: *Epoch and Artist*
New York 1959, page 12

2
John Summerson: *Heavenly Mansions*
page 197

3
James S. Ackerman
The Architecture of Michelangelo
London 1961, page 139

4
T. S. Eliot
Use of Poetry and Use of Criticism
Cambridge, Mass. 1933, page 146

5
Anita Brookner
The Genius of the Future
London 1971, page 21

6
Phil Virden
The Social Determinants of Aesthetic Styles
British Journal of Aesthetics, 1971

7
S. E. Hyman: *The Armed Vision*
New York 1955, page 237

8
William Empson
Seven Types of Ambiguity
London 1930, page 174

9
Cleanth Brooks
The Well Wrought Urn
New York 1947, pages 212–14

10
Edmund W. Sinnott
The Problem of Organic Form
New Haven 1963

Intention and response

1
Wladyslaw Tatarkiewicz
What is art? The Problem of Definition Today
British Journal of Aesthetics, 1971
pages 134–52

2
Anita Brookner: *The Genius of the Future*
London 1971, page 21

3
Loc. cit., page 22

4
Freart de Chambray
Parallele de l'architecture antique et de la moderne
Paris 1702 (first ed. 1650)

5
Wolfgang Hermann
Laugier and 18th Century French Theory
London 1962

6
M. Wietz
The Role of Theory in Aesthetics
Problems in Aesthetics, ed. M. Wietz
New York 1959

Playing the environment cool

1
Phil Virden
The Social Determinants of Aesthetic Styles
British Journal of Aesthetics, Spring 1972

2
Zdzistaw Kowalski
The Meaning and Future of Architecture
Poland Magazine, No.7, 1972, page 21

3
Marshall McLuhan: *Understanding Media*
London 1964

The architect as an open-ended system

1
[1]In 1972 British architects were asked to redefine the role of their institute, the Royal Institute of British Architects, by giving weighting and priority to a list of possible functions provided by Council. These possible functions were given as: (a) a club (mainly social); (b) a society for promoting architectural excellence; (c) a learned society (in the historical sense); (d) a 'trade union'; (e) a lobby (in the political sense); (f) a spearhead of radical change; (g) a society for promoting architectural competence; (h) a society of architecture (as opposed to architects); (i) an institute of the 'built environment' (embracing all environmental professions and interests in a combined club/lobby format); (j) a centre for active learning.

(c) A learned society and (j) a centre for active learning should be indistinguishable and both would appear to be prerequisites for (f). Also (g) being concerned with competence is similarly a prerequisite for (b). In (i) the existence of the institute itself is brought in question as is the existence of any guiding principles for the practice of architecture. The general confusion about standards of competence and excellence as evidenced by architects' failure to be sufficiently aware of published research results (see the Building Research Station *Annual Report 1962* and Brick Development Association technical note Vol. 1, No. 4, 1971, on the failure of brick cladding in multi-storey framed structures) suggests that the creation of a 'trade union' would bring with it a form of legalized acceptance of declining standards of performance already characteristic of other 'trades'.

Among other issues raised by the debate was the fact that the statutory obligation for the Institute to be a learned society had not been brought in line with an effective promotion and dissemination of active learning. The enthusiasm and vigour with which the question of role has been debated, however, suggests that the list has at least provided a check for members' values and aspirations. It gives some room, moreover, for optimism on the part of the consumer.

2
Frank Kermode: *The Sense of an Ending*
London 1970

3
Published by HMSO, London 1969

4
Karl Popper
The Open Society and its Enemies, volume 1
London 1945

5
Serge Chermayeff and Christopher Alexander
Community and Privacy
London 1963

6
William Barrett: *Irrational Man*
New York, 1958, page 39

7
Ibid., page 47

8
In origin it has nothing to do with either elephants or castles. The name in fact derives from the Cockney mispronunciation of the Spanish *Infanta de Castiglia*

Contexts for the future of architecture

1
Wilem Frischmann and Malcolm Quantrill
The Dual Use of land in central urban areas
Public Works Congress, London,
November 1972

2
Strip City, *Architectural Design*
April 1970, page 178

3
Boulevard cities: studies in the replanning of Paris and Berlin
Architectural Design, May 1968

4
Architectural Design
March 1970, pages 140–5

5
Richard and Su Rogers with Design
Research Unit
Zip-up enclosures, *Architectural Design*
March 1970; pages 146–7

6
Straits of Messina Road/Rail Link
Architectural Design, May 1970
pages 228–9

7
Seaborne Airport
Architectural Design, March 1970
page 125

8
Atmosfield and Atmosraft
Architectural Design, March 1972
pages 169–70

9
See Barry Commoner: *The Closing Circle*
London 1972, pages 125–215

10
Inflatable cathedral for San José, Costa Rica
by the Firestone Tyre and Rubber Company
Architectural Design, February 1970
page 57

11
Cedric Price and Frank Newby
Air structures: a survey
London 1971

Index